The Adventurous Heart

The Adventurous Heart

Second Edition

Figures and Capriccios

Ernst Jünger

Translated by Thomas Friese

Edited by Russell A. Berman

With an Introduction by Eliah Bures and Elliot Neaman

Telos Press Publishing
Candor, NY

Printed in the United States of America
16 15 14 13 12 1 2 3 4

Translated by permission from the German original, *Das Abenteuerliche Herz: Figuren und Capriccios* (2nd edition, 1938) and "Sizilischer Brief an den Mann im Mond" (1930), in Ernst Jünger, *Sämtliche Werke*, vol. 9, pp. 177–330 and 9–22, Stuttgart 1979.

ISBN: 978-0-914386-48-3

Library of Congress Cataloging-in-Publication Data

Jünger, Ernst, 1895-1998.
[Abenteuerliche Herz. English]
The adventurous heart : figures and capriccios / Ernst Jünger ; translated by Thomas Friese ; edited by Russell A. Berman ; with an introduction by Eliah Bures and Elliot Neaman.
p. cm.
Translation of the 2nd German language ed., 1938.
Includes bibliographical references.
ISBN 978-0-914386-48-3 (alk. paper)
I. Berman, Russell A., 1950- II. Title.
PT2619.U43A713 2012
838'.91207—dc23

2012025830

Telos Press Publishing
20 Main Street
Candor, NY 13743

www.telospress.com

Contents

Translator's Preface

With this first English translation of *Das Abenteuerliche Herz, Zweite Fassung* now complete, I gladly leave a formal introduction to the expertise of Elliot Neaman and Eliah Bures. Let me at once add how grateful I am to Elliot, Eliah, and Russell Berman of Telos Press for conceiving and realizing this important project—a new English translation of a Jünger work was more than overdue. It is indeed remarkable, inexplicable, that so much of one of Germany's most important authors still remains untranslated into the world's new *lingua franca*—particularly as this is not the case for other important languages.

For myself, I would only add a few words here on the importance of this particular work being available in English, particularly for new Jünger readers.

Indeed, I myself encountered Jünger twenty years ago through this book, in Italian translation, at a reading group of the Association Eumeswil in Florence. I had never heard of Jünger, but this book hooked me on the author for life.

In retrospect, I understand my good fortune in having had a direct and naïve encounter with the original source. Far too many readers and students, when they eventually arrive at reading Jünger first-hand (and not merely critiques of his life or works), have difficulty in overcoming the simplistic and extremely incomplete stereotypes that have passively deposited in them from decades of mostly politically motivated commentaries on some early works. In reality, Jünger was nothing if not an author in continuous and ascending evolution. His thought and writings developed for literally seven decades (!) after *Storm of Steel* (1920), *Battle as Inner Experience* (1922), and *The Worker* (1932), and, moreover, decisively in the direction of *apolitea*.

Thus, unfortunately, the rich and diverse world of mature Jüngerian thought remains unknown to many: beginning with this work of 1938, through his allegory on tyranny, *On the Marble Cliffs* (1939), his peace plea, *The Peace* (1943), written and secretly circulated during World War II, his prophetic work on technology, *The Glass Bees* (1957), his long essay on his varied drug experiences, *Annäherungen: Drogen und Rausch* (1970), the various years of diaries (*Strahlungen*), through many other works, to the great compendium of mature Jüngerian thought, *Eumeswil* (1977)...and then on for another three productive decades to his death in 1998 at the age of 102!

If the present work begins the truly valuable phase of Jünger's writings, fortunately it is also the best introduction to Jünger for new readers. Its format and content are uniquely effective in introducing in a concise and captivating manner the most important Jüngerian themes, which the author then elaborated and developed over the next six decades. And although some objective background in the biographical and socio-political reality in which Jünger wrote this work will broaden the reader's understanding, its most crucial messages are thoroughly comprehensible without any prior knowledge at all; in fact, the socio-political and biographical context, if they become the main thing, can even distract from the deeper value of the work.

What is critical is a certain direct application of the reader's own intelligence, intuition, and life experiences. The reader's real task, where he will make his richest spoils, is to grasp for himself, to interiorize the actual experience or reflection that Jünger relates. Read that way, this little volume can open our own hearts to the many adventures hidden in our lives where they are most thoroughly concealed: directly before our eyes, in the everyday (and every-night) world. As the author says in "In the Shops (2)":

> ...we often take off on remarkable detours seeking out in distant peoples and forgotten times arrangements that surround us seamlessly on all sides. It takes a long time before we realize that we have been superbly equipped with our two eyes and that the nearest street corner suffices to observe all these curious things.

I cannot wish the reader any more valuable result than precisely this realization. If the book also serves as an opening into the greater world of Jüngerian thought, all the better.

In conclusion, I wish to thank my wife Ioanna for her emotional support, the members of the Association Eumeswil for introducing me to Jünger and discussing the essential meanings of this book, Roland Knappe at Klett-Cotta for granting Telos Press the translation rights, and Eliah Bures for his valuable feedback on my translation.

May it be only the first in a new phase of Jünger translations into English!

Thomas Friese

INTRODUCTION

Eliah Bures and Elliot Neaman

Regarding the *Figures and Capriccios*, I would like to say the following. As far as the closeness of observation is concerned, I prefer a piece like "In the Shops".... It gives the reader a model of how to use his eye and sets him to thinking, since he has to see that here a wide field has been left for his own observations. The pleasure in such a piece also derives from the recognition it provides that the world, for the spiritual person, always remains *terra incognita*. Such acts of exploration increase one's feeling of freedom.

Friedrich Georg Jünger[1]

I believe myself here to be taking that leveling through which the world appears at once simpler and more miraculous a decisive step further. It's a question of the complete presence and unity of the spirit by day and night, in waking and in dreaming, in all borders and boundlessness, in all states of matter and illusion. I have managed, I think, to find a model for this; no doubt it was only possible in this abbreviated fashion, since otherwise whole libraries would not have sufficed. I want to wield prose with a new potency and push it to the edge of enchantment. In this last year...I believe to have penetrated into domains that no one before me has seen.

Ernst Jünger[2]

I

What kinds of human beings have adventurous hearts? Persons led more by intuition or instinct than by reason? Persons for whom to avoid

1. Friedrich Georg Jünger to Ernst Jünger, December 25, 1937, A: Ernst Jünger, Deutsches Literaturarchiv Marbach (hereafter DLAM). All translations are ours unless otherwise noted.

2. Ernst Jünger to Friedrich Georg Jünger, January 6, 1938, D: Friedrich Georg Jünger, DLAM.

danger is to accept boredom? Adventure, perhaps the oldest of all literary genres, is a key that can unlock many of Ernst Jünger's writings. Gerhard Nebel, who worked as a translator in Paris in 1941, and was a lifelong friend, latched on to the concept in an early post–World War II reception, describing Jünger's spiritual and metaphysical thirst for adventure as the glue that holds together such disparate endeavors as militant nationalism and Christian spiritualism.[3] Gerhard Loose picked up the adventure theme in his Jünger biography, emphasizing the pitfalls inherent in the *culte de moi* of the author (*ichbezogenheit*), which reduces the natural world, foreign lands, war, just about any phenomenon, to objects of speculation for Jünger's aesthetic imagination.[4]

In Jünger's novels, the hero frequently trades the familiarity of the known for the strangeness and risks of the unknown. This impulse was the driving force of the young Ernst Jünger's escape fantasies, which were finally satisfied by the biggest adventure of them all, the Great War. *The Adventurous Heart*, which appeared in 1929 with the subtitle "Sketches by Day and Night," and then in a heavily edited new version in 1938 with the subtitle "Figures and Capriccios," was his only work to explicitly use the term in the title. In the latter version, Jünger presents the reader with sixty-three short, apparently arbitrary and unrelated un-dated diary entries. Both books seemed insignificant at the time of publication and did not sell well. In hindsight, though, we see that already in its first version, this small volume marked the point at which the developing writer expanded his horizon from being a chronicler of the First World War to an author and thinker with a much wider range and deeper grasp. He lived to the biblical age of one hundred and two, publishing diaries to the end that retain the style and method first worked out in this book and in a short, imaginative piece from 1930, here also translated as "Sicilian Letter to the Man in the Moon."

The second edition of *The Adventurous Heart* marks another important turning point. Though Jünger would remain a world traveler throughout his life, by 1938 he had given up on the external adventurous experience in favor of an internal exploration of consciousness. The split resulted from a gradual evolutionary process. In 1922 he edited out

3. Gerhard Nebel, *Ernst Jünger: Abenteuer des Geistes* (Wuppertal: Marées, 1949).

4. Gerhard Loose, *Ernst Jünger: Gestalt und Werk* (Frankfurt am Main: Klostermann, 1957).

the psychological observations on war from his famous first book, *Storm of Steel*, and put them into a separately published essay, *Battle as Inner Experience*. But years of explicit political activity followed. He was regarded as one of the leaders of a "new nationalism," composed of young, battle-tested veterans fighting an even larger global battle of ideas in the 1920s. National Socialism was obviously one of those big ideas, but not the only one.

Jünger believed that Hitler was only one leader of this new nationalism, a good drummer perhaps, who pointed the way to the future, but not the inevitable redeemer of Germany. In 1926 he sent Hitler a copy of his *Fire and Blood* with the revealingly ambiguous inscription, "To the Nationalist Führer, Adolf Hitler."[5] Jünger seemed to believe that he could leave it to the National Socialists to organize the masses while he and other intellectuals of the new generation would band together to form an elite ideological corps, modeled on the Jesuits or medieval knights, who would shape a New Germany. It didn't take long after Hitler seized power for him to see that these ideas were dangerously romantic and illusory. He was offered a seat in the Reichstag and in the newly Nazified Prussian Academy of the Arts. He declined both. The 1938 version of *The Adventurous Heart* marks a clear and final break with this nationalist phase, from the style of writing alone.

He had been a hero for the Nazis. He was left alone by the Gestapo (except for one house search) because Hitler regarded him as one of the war's greatest heroes. Goebbels called *Storm of Steel* a "war gospel, truly great," but he was utterly disappointed by the first version of *The Adventurous Heart*; it was "just ink, literature," he scoffed.[6] When the *Völkischer Beobachter* nevertheless published some excerpts from the book, Jünger wrote a scathing letter to the editors, scolding them for having published his work without permission.

What Goebbels and many others on the right didn't understand was that for Jünger politics was only one form of adventure. Etymologically the word derives from the Latin *advenire*, to happen or to have something happen. The adventurer puts herself in a situation where the

5. The copy is in the Library of Congress; see Elliot Y. Neaman, *A Dubious Past: The Politics of Literature after Nazism* (Berkeley: Univ. of California Press, 1999), p. 31. "The nationalist leader" could mean the only one, or just one of many.

6. Joseph Goebbels, *Die Tagebücher von Joseph Goebbels: Sämtliche Fragmente*, ed. Elke Fröhlich (Munich: Saur, 1987), see April 4, 1929.

unexpected, the dangerous can occur. The adventurer steps out of the known order, out of the traditional rules and travels without insurance or protection. Jünger was by disposition unable to follow the standard rules. As a boy he was very curious and intelligent, but he did poorly in school. He daydreamed and chafed at the strict methods of the Wilhelmine schoolmasters. He joined the Wandervögel, a youth organization that rebelled against the dull routine of bourgeois life by escaping into the woods, camping out, singing newly discovered folk songs to an accompanying guitar. Even that was too tame for the restless teenager. He had read everything he could get his hands on about equatorial Africa. In order to get there, he ran away from his last year of high school. In November 1913, at age eighteen, he made his way to Verdun, told recruiters he was twenty (the minimum age for enlistment), joined the Foreign Legion, and was shipped off to Algeria from Marseilles, with the intention of deserting and exploring the dark continent of his fantasies.

The boy's African plan never succeeded. He did escape from camp with a few co-adventurers, but they were caught, rounded up, and shipped back to the base. Meanwhile, his father had secured his release through the German embassy. The whole adventure lasted two months. The father treated the affair as a boyish prank. He made sure Ernstel had a photo taken in a studio in Sidi Bel-Abbès. The portrait shows him with an impish grin, holding cap and belt in his Foreign Legion uniform.

The father was not only lenient; he offered to take his son on a return trip to Africa once he finished his high school exams. Then fate intervened, as the guns of August beckoned. For Jünger's generation, the First World War started off, of course, as a welcome relief from the stultifying atmosphere of an overly complacent and joyless world. Trainloads of excited youngsters headed off to the front on packed trains, mothers, sisters, and sweethearts throwing flowers after them. Most expected to return by Christmas, victorious.

Even when two years later the last of these illusions died in the rat-infested trenches of Verdun and the Somme, Jünger, though susceptible to bouts of frustration and despair, never stopped viewing the war as a great adventure.[7] He made copious notes and published them in diary

7. That Jünger fully registered the war's grim absurdities is clear from his original war diaries; long inaccessible to scholars, they have recently been published as

form as *Storm of Steel* in 1920. The book went through numerous revisions, evolving from schoolboy jottings in the style of a Homeric tale of war to sophisticated observations about the nature of war itself. In hindsight, we see already developing Jünger's tendency to separate the surface events, we might say the phenomena, from the underlying noumena, or significance of the events in a cosmic sense. Where other writers wrote against the war (Barbusse) or about the lost generation that experienced and survived the war (Remarque), Jünger believed that he was witnessing a shift in the entire global culture, the end of heroic individuals replaced by their subjugation to the machine. The battles he describes are written from a phenomenologically neutral perspective, as if he were witnessing a natural catastrophe, like an earthquake or a fire, but each example has a larger significance for culture and history.

This morphological view, derived from deep reading of Nietzsche and especially Spengler, translated into his taking sides in the ideological battles of the 1920s and early 1930s. Jünger felt called upon to read and translate for his generation the deeper meaning of the crisis of his time. That crisis, he was convinced, came from the fact that the war had washed away the last remnants of nineteenth-century bourgeois liberalism, but the new era was still up for grabs. One needed to face the fact with hardened, "heroic realism" but also as a participant in the "total mobilization" of a new soldier/worker society.

The 1929 version of *The Adventurous Heart* is a more pessimistic, culturally despairing work, in line with Jünger's politics and activities of the period. The inspiration for the title and, to a certain extent, the style of the book can be attributed to the publication of *Le Paysan de Paris* (translated by Frederick Brown as *Nightwalker*), a popular book published in 1926 by the twenty-six-year-old Louis Aragon.[8] The book, dedicated to the surrealist André Masson, is a whirlwind tour through

Kriegstagebuch: 1914–1918 (Stuttgart: Klett-Cotta, 2010). As he remarked in the entry for May 24, 1917, with a characteristic longing for *other* adventures: "When will this shitty war come to an end? What couldn't one have seen and enjoyed during this time. . . . But still no end in sight. The whole business is becoming hellishly monotonous."

8. The title appears taken from a passage in which Aragon, writing against "all the dogmatic and realistic forces of the world," summons an army of "solemn and adventurous hearts indifferent to victory who seek, at night, a chasm down which to hurl yourselves." See Louis Aragon, *Nightwalker*, trans. Frederick Brown (Engelwood Cliffs: Prentice Hall, 1970), pp. 53–54.

the streets of the city of light, often at night, focusing on the magical sights and sounds and odd figures who populate the demimonde. Walter Benjamin, who was inspired by the volume to begin work on his *Arcades Project*, claimed to have been unable to "read more than two or three pages at a time, for my heartbeat became so strong that I was forced to lay the book down."[9] Aragon filled these pages with rambling thoughts and collage-like observations, poetic, philosophical, and literary. There are two long sections devoted to the wide Boulevard Haussmann of the Opéra, and a large park, the Buttes Chaumont, whose distinguishing feature is a lake upon which perched a hilly island featuring a temple dedicated to the prophetic priestess Sybil. In the preface, Aragon speculated about modern mythology and introduced the idea of uncovering marvels from everyday events:

> I am truly beginning to experience awareness that neither the senses nor reason can, except by deceit, be understood separately, and that they undoubtedly exist only as functions. The consummate triumph of reason, beyond discoveries, surprises, and improbabilities, lies in its ratification of some commonly held myth. Its consummate glory lies in finding exact meaning for those expressions of the instinct which the half-wise formerly spurned.[10]

This manifesto-like assertion of the primacy of myth and instinct over reason fairly well describes Jünger's project in *The Adventurous Heart* and in his writings in general. Some observers have called Jünger's method a forerunner of "magical realism." His key contribution was the "stereoscopic" view, which he introduced in the first edition. Building up to the idea, he reflects on a note made by his primary school teacher on his report card of "insufficient concentration," followed by the thought that he had discovered a way of relating to the world, which accompanied all his years, by disconnecting, dis-involving, dis-attaching from reality, but at the same time re-connecting, the way a spider attaches itself with webs to the world.[11] This reorientation constitutes

9. Quoted in Richard Wolin, *Walter Benjamin: An Aesthetic of Redemption* (Berkeley and Los Angeles: Univ. of California Press, 1994), p. 128.

10. Aragon, *Nightwalker*, p. 4.

11. Ernst Jünger, *Das abenteuerliche Herz* (Erste Fassung), in *Sämtliche Werke* (Stuttgart: Klett-Cotta, 1978–2003), 9:51. This is a gloss on the passage, not Jünger's

the *adventure* of the book's title, for example exploring unknown lands like Robinson Crusoe, getting lost in nature museums, or in the final adventure, death, the "greatest and most dangerous of them all."[12] This means of dis-involvement leads inevitably to different perceptions of reality, one of which we might call "poetic synesthesia," the delineation of separate sensual qualities in an object. The "stereoscopic perception" (*Sinnlichkeit*), he tells us, means "extracting two sensual qualities from one and the same object, through, and this is essential, the same sense organ."[13] One sense organ has to take over a function of another. Thus a red, fragrant carnation is not stereoscopic, involving merely sight and smell separately. But a velvet carnation that emits the fragrance of cinnamon is stereoscopic, because the nose both smells and tastes the qualities of spice simultaneously. The device has roots in French decadence and symbolism, as evidenced by repeated occurrences in the poems of Arthur Rimbaud and Charles Baudelaire.[14] Another good example is the famous J. K. Huysmans novel, *À Rebours*, called by some the *summa* of the decadent imagination. The story concerns the neurasthenic aristocrat des Esseintes, who furnishes a strange villa that includes a "liquor organ." Des Esseintes tells us:

> Each and every liquor, in his opinion, corresponded in taste with the sound of a particular instrument. Dry curaçao, for instance, was like the clarinet with its piercing, velvety note; kümmel like the oboe with its sonorous, nasal timbre; crème de menthe and anisette like the flute, at once sweet and tart, soft and shrill...[15]

exact words. Later he will apply the French phrase "désinvolture" to describe this way of being in the world.

12. Ibid., p. 72.

13. Ibid., p. 83.

14. See Baudelaire's "Correspondences," from 1857: "There are perfumes fresh like the skin of infants, / Sweet like oboes, green like prairies / —And others corrupted, rich and triumphant." Rimbaud was even more explicit in "Vowels": "A black, E white, I red, U green, O blue: vowels, / I shall tell, one day, of your mysterious origins: / A, black velvety jacket of brilliant flies / which buzz around cruel smells..." Charles Baudelaire, "Correspondances" ("Correspondences"), in *Flowers of Evil* (Oxford: Oxford UP, 2008), p. 18; Arthur Rimbaud, "Voyelles" ("Vowels"), in *Rimbaud: Complete Works, Selected Letters: A Bilingual Edition* (Chicago: Univ. of Chicago Press, 2005), p. 140.

15. J. K. Huysmans, *Against Nature*, trans. Robert Baldick (New York: Penguin, 1959), p. 58.

Jünger's intense interest in the materiality of language, trying to fulfill, perhaps, what Rimbaud promised when he wrote of vowels, "I shall tell, one day, of your mysterious origins,"[16] is evident in the essay "In Praise of Vowels," published in a 1934 anthology entitled *Leaves and Stones*.[17] This collection of eight works did contain the polemical essay "Total Mobilization," but it was otherwise characterized by more reflective, literary pieces, including "On Pain" and the aforementioned "Sicilian Letter to the Man in the Moon."

For Jünger vowels belong to a higher metaphysical order than consonants, and among the vowels he detects an internal hierarchical ladder, each rung related to certain spatial, social, and color characteristics. *A*, for example, is the "king of vowels," which expresses height and width, while *O* is the aristocracy, spanning height and depths.[18] We mention these philological investigations to make the point that in the first years of the Nazi dictatorship, Jünger's interests were often far removed from the politics of the day. An expectation existed that writers under the new regime would coordinate their work with what Victor Klemperer called *lingua tertii imperii*.[19] Clearly Jünger felt no inclination to do so, and by ignoring the new speech code he could be seen as registering a not insignificant gesture of resistance. Moreover, the epigrams that conclude this collection, written in 1933–34, contain barely veiled critiques of the regime, with references to the "mob" (*Pöbel*), "the demos is its own tyranny," and to the methods of the new state: "Slavery increases notably when one accords it the appearance of freedom."[20]

Jünger turned his back on the revolution in Germany in more literal ways too. He spent much of the summer of 1935 in Norway; in October 1936 he embarked on a steamship voyage to the Brazilian Amazon, with a stopover in the Canary Islands; and in April 1938 he left again, this time for Rhodes—all journeys recorded in subsequently published diaries. What's more, in the summer of 1937 Jünger traveled to Paris, where he met with the French writers André Gide and Jean Schlumberger, who had founded the elite modernist journal *Nouvelle Revue*

16. Rimbaud, "Voyelles," p. 140.

17. Ernst Jünger, *Blätter und Steine* (Hamburg: Hanseatische Verlagsanstalt, 1934).

18. Ernst Jünger, "Lob der Vokale," in *Sämtliche* Werke, 12:34–35.

19. Victor Klemperer, *Language of the Third Reich*, trans. Martin Brady (London: Continuum, 2000).

20. Ernst Jünger, "Epigramme," in *Sämtliche Werke*, 12:510, 512.

Française, as well as with the French-American Julien Green and the German authors Annette Kolb and Joseph Breitbach, whose books were banned during the Third Reich. These connections helped integrate him into a wide network of French intellectuals, launching his reputation in France, where he was always more revered and appreciated than in his native country.

No less significant was the decision, taken in 1936, to resettle his family from Goslar in the Harz to Überlingen on Lake Constance, whence one could view freer lands to the south. The same year *African Games* appeared, a novel that fictionalized his youthful adventure as a foreign legionnaire in Algeria.[21] He retells here the tales of his two unsuccessful escapes. Significantly the novel ends with a tone of resignation and farewell to youthful adventure: "We are born a little too wild, and cure the seething fever with drinks of the bitter kind."[22]

Fearing war and preferring to serve, if necessary, in his old regiment, Jünger moved again in April 1939, this time to Kirchhorst, near Hannover, where he finished the novel *On the Marble Cliffs*. The book appeared in print in October, just as he was being conscripted into the Wehrmacht, promoted to captain, and ordered to the Western Front. Jünger had been offered a foreign diplomatic post by Foreign Minister Joachim von Ribbentrop, but he declined.[23] The novel is a thinly veiled portrait of Jünger and his younger brother Friedrich Georg, as well as an allegory of the descent of Germany into totalitarianism. The story takes place on a fantasy landscape, with an urban coastal area on one side and flatlands on the other, populated by farmers and herdsmen. In the middle a striking mountain of marble cliffs overlooks the entire area. The two brothers have resigned from the "Mauretanians," a militia made up of rough veterans, and have retreated to the isolation of a house built in the marble cliffs, where they pursue botanical studies and enjoy the leisure to read and daydream. This idyll is interrupted by the appearance of a violent intruder, the Chief Ranger, who is bent on

21. Stuart Hood translated the book in 1954 as *African Diversions* (London: J. Lehmann). But as Gerhard Loose notes, "play" or "games" is the right word, for Jünger considered himself a *homo ludens*, a man liberated from normal social responsibilities, free to pursue his inclinations wherever they might lead.

22. Ernst Jünger, *Afrikanische Spiele*, in *Sämtliche Werke*, 15:245.

23. Heimo Schwilk, ed., *Ernst Jünger: Leben und Werk in Bildern und Texten* (Stuttgart: Klett-Cotta, 1988), p. 316.

destroying this peaceful, urban civilization. The interloper is challenged by various heroic figures, who represent the German church and aristocracy, but they are defeated. The Chief Ranger even has a special site, Köppels-Bleek, a kind of concentration camp reserved for his captives, where the prisoners are tortured and then their bleached heads arrayed on poles as a warning to the others.

How the Nazis allowed this novel to be published is a bit of a mystery. Even with paper shortages, twenty thousand copies were printed for the armed forces in 1943.[24] Documents that surfaced in the 1970s appear to substantiate the widely held belief that Hitler himself protected Jünger and ordered that nothing be done to stop publication, even though many high-ranking Nazis were upset, including Goebbels, who saw himself caricatured as Braquemart, one of the Chief Ranger's rivals in the novel.[25] It is also important to note that the above summary of the plot highlights the obvious connections to contemporaneous political events, while in fact Jünger did a good job of concealing any direct political translation of the story by means of mystical visions, surrealistic descriptions, and symbolic allegories. Years later he even denied that it was a novel of opposition.[26] Be that as it may, the book has gone down in literary history as an exemplary product of the German inner emigration.

Jünger kept a diary again for the entirety of the Second World War, in addition to three years of occupation by the allied forces. The first part, *Gardens and Streets*, was published in 1942. The book covered the invasion of France, in which Jünger participated as an infantry officer. The work was later censored and afterward denied paper for any further publications. The rest of the diaries were eventually published under the collective title *Strahlungen* (*Radiations*), denoting perhaps the radioactive flash of Hiroshima, or magic lanterns, or as he himself writes in the preface, the complex impressions produced by the world and its objects, the way that light passing through a lattice divides into patterns of shadow and light. In other words the title encompasses ambiguity, the gray zone, where paradoxes and uncertainties ruled the world since the First World War.[27]

24. Gerhard Loose, *Ernst Jünger* (New York: Twayne, 1974), p. 62.
25. Neaman, *A Dubious Past*, p. 113.
26. See the postscript to the 1973 Ullstein edition.
27. Ernst Jünger, *Strahlungen I*, in *Sämtliche Werke*, 2:14–15.

Following the fall of France, Jünger was ensconced in Paris's Hotel Majestic, on the Avenue Kléber, where the staff of the German occupation forces were housed. The second and fourth parts of the diary cover his activities there, written in secret and kept in a hotel safe. The third part of the diary was published as *Caucasian Sketches*. They record a trip made in the fall of 1942 to early 1943 to the Eastern Front, where the key turning point in the war, the Battle of Stalingrad, was in progress. Jünger's commander in Paris, General Carl-Heinrich von Stülpnagel, was involved in the German resistance and wanted a first-hand, unvarnished account of the war against the Soviets. Stülpnagel played an integral part in the Stauffenberg plot to assassinate Hitler on July 20, 1944. Thinking that Hitler was dead, he rounded up all the SS and Gestapo agents in Paris on that day. He tried to commit suicide but only succeeded in wounding himself and was later sentenced to death and hanged by piano wire at the infamous Plötzensee prison. Though under suspicion, Jünger was able to avoid the bloody reprisals after July 20; he was, however, discharged from his duties in Paris and spent the last months of the war behind the "Siegfried Line," with young boys and old men who offered final but useless resistance to the allied forces entering Germany. The record of these months was called the *Kirchhorst Pages*. All five diaries were published in 1949 as *Strahlungen*. Later, in 1962, the final diary, *A Cottage in the Vineyard*, which covered the years 1945 to 1948 and whose title alluded to the prophet Isaiah's pronouncement of richly deserved ruin (see Isaiah 1:7–8), was added to *Strahlungen* in the first *Collected Works*.

In Paris Jünger had an unchallenging job as a mail censor. In his spare time, which was considerable, he browsed through museums, antique shops, and bookstores. Besides collecting art and books, he nurtured contacts with famous writers and artists in Paris. In the salon of Marie-Louise Bousquet, he came into contact with "l'Hitlerisme Français," with Pierre Drieu la Rochelle and Henri de Montherlant. Through the ambassador to Bucharest, Paul Morand, he met Benoist Méchin, who belonged to the Vichy government, and Ferdinand Céline, the fascist sympathizer. But he also frequented the salon of Florence Gould (Lady Orphington in the diaries),[28] where he rubbed shoulders with

28. Florence Gould had various pseudonyms; see Allan Mitchell, *The Devil's Captain: Ernst Jünger in Nazi Paris, 1941–1944* (New York: Berghahn, 2011), pp. 82–84. Our

Braques, Picasso, Sacha Guitry, Julien Gracq, Paul Léautaud, and Jean Paulhan, one of the founders of the resistance newspaper *Lettres Françaises.*[29] Jünger kept his distance from the various resistance plots that were brewing among a group of officers, led by Stülpnagel, who met in secret at the hotel George V. He didn't trust the generals, who had made a personal oath to Hitler, to be able to carry out a coup. On July 20, he spent the day hunting butterflies in the Bois de Boulogne. Jean Cocteau said it best: "Some people have dirty hands, some have clean hands, but Jünger had no hands."[30]

Besides the secret diaries, during the war Jünger also worked on an essay that was published in Amsterdam in 1946, after being denied publication rights by the occupation authorities. It was called *The Peace.* In this unapologetic, religiously infused essay, Jünger conceives of the period from 1918 to 1945 as a long European civil war. He discusses the explosion of technology that brings with it an exponential increase in the ability to create destruction. He writes of the failure of the League of Nations and the harsh terms of the Versailles Treaty. The victors, he warns, should not take revenge on the vanquished. The war was won by one side, he intones, but the peace must be won by all. History is represented as a vale of tears and all of mankind as equal subjects of suffering, the line between victim and victimizer erased. Jünger had read the Bible twice during the war years, both Old and New Testaments, from beginning to end. *The Peace* is imbued with a Christian sense that the new world must be accompanied by a religious revival, the only means to conquer the nihilism of the previous decades.

With the publication of *The Peace* in 1946, and *Strahlungen* in 1949, began *Der Fall Jünger*, a series of debates and controversies about his life and works that lasted throughout his career and continues after his death. Typically, the appearance of one of his books would be greeted by an enthusiastic review, followed by storms of indignation, or the other way around, by a biting, vociferous critique, followed by a fire wall

thanks are due to Allan Mitchell for comments and corrections on a late draft of this introduction.

29. On his contacts to the collaborators and to the resistance, see Neaman, *A Dubious Past*, pp. 143–44.

30. See Thomas Nevin, *Ernst Jünger and Germany: Into the Abyss, 1914–1945* (Durham, NC: Duke UP, 1996), p. 169.

of apologetics. The arguments were often carried out in an ideological manner, reflecting the political point of view of the respective reviewer. But in hindsight, one can see that Jünger's provocation was so deep because, like those rays of light and darkness, he was so hard to pin down. He reflected the ambiguities, the horrible lows, and the redemptive highs of German history in the twentieth century from the long perspective. To this aspect of Jünger's life and work we now turn.

II

The Romanian-born American literary critic Virgil Nemoianu recently summed up Jünger's "somewhat puzzling and ambiguous" current reputation:

> By every reasonable standard—historical impact, breadth and depth of philosophical and aesthetic vision, variety of work, responsiveness to cultural-historical evolutions—he ought to be placed at the highest level of literary/aesthetic achievement. In fact he is thus judged and recognized in many parts of the world, for instance, in France, Spain, Romania, and South America. By contrast, in Anglo-Saxon lands and in his home country critical reactions often range from studied ignorance and thin-lipped distaste to intense hostility and severe accusations: thus, a few years ago the influential critic Geoffrey Hartman roundly called Jünger "a Nazi thinker."[31]

There is no need to dwell on the German role in this strikingly lopsided reception.[32] Suffice it to note that calling Jünger "controversial" has long been an obligatory cliché among German pundits. (The dispute's most public flare-up was undoubtedly the commotion caused by Jünger's receipt, in 1982, of the city of Frankfurt am Main's prestigious Goethe Prize, though the debate over Jünger's earlier ties to fascism—and his lingering illiberal commitments—was already decades old.) Instead, let us merely sample in passing from the sneers of some of Jünger's more august contemporaries. Thomas Mann, for one, deemed him "an ice-cold

31. Virgil Nemoianu, *Postmodernism and Cultural Identities: Conflicts and Coexistence* (Washington, DC: Catholic Univ. of America Press, 2010), p. 286.

32. For the most sustained account of the Jünger reception, see Neaman, *A Dubious Past*. A concise overview can be found in Steffen Martus, *Ernst Jünger* (Stuttgart and Weimar: J. B. Metzler, 2001), pp. 3–11, 167–78.

playboy of barbarism,"[33] while Walter Benjamin famously lampooned the "boyish rapture" and "utterly thoughtless obtuseness" of Jünger's "cult of war."[34] To Theodor Adorno, Jünger was quite simply a "nauseating fellow."[35] And Hans-Ulrich Wehler, doyen of the so-called Bielefeld school of history, judged Jünger among the "greatest criminals of modern German cultural history"[36]—an estimation itself characteristic of countless rancorous appraisals from left-leaning academics during the forty-one years of the West German republic. The official party line on Jünger from communist East Germany, it goes without saying, was to place him unceremoniously and without a trace of nuance into the camp of fascists and militarists who helped prepare an entire generation for the coming of National Socialism.[37]

To be sure, more appreciative voices, sometimes from the unlikeliest quarters, are not hard to find. Erich Marie Remarque, a year before publishing *All Quiet on the Western Front* (1929), praised Jünger's own celebrated—and far more bellicose—accounts of the First World War as books "of a beneficial objectivity, precise, serious, intense, and powerful." The playwright Carl Zuckmayer, whose works were banned by the Nazis and who spent the Second World War in exile in the United States, wrote in a 1943 secret report for the Office of Strategic Services that Jünger was "by far the most talented and important of the writers to have remained in Germany." Jünger's opposition to the Nazi regime, Zuckmayer insisted, was on a spiritual plane: "[His] glorification of war has nothing to do with aggression or plans for world domination—his ideal of a superior man nothing to do with the demagogic nonsense of a master 'race.'" "As regards thought, content, and style," Zuckmayer

33. Thomas Mann to Agnes E. Meyer, December 14, 1945, in *Thomas Mann: Briefe, 1937–1947*, ed. Erika Mann (Berlin and Weimar: Aufbau, 1965), p. 495.

34. Walter Benjamin, "Theories of German Fascism," trans. Jerold Wikoff, *New German Critique* 17 (Spring 1979): 121–22.

35. Quoted in Klaus Modick, "Präsenz und Einheit," *Die Zeit*, March 10, 1989.

36. Quoted in Helmuth Kiesel, *Ernst Jünger: Die Biographie* (Munich: Siedler, 2007), p. 16.

37. An excellent example was Wolfgang Harich, who wrote a dyspeptic attack on Jünger in the East German flagship periodical *Der Aufbau* in 1946. Harich had a checkered past, having worked in Ribbentrop's foreign ministry during the war, but during the occupation became a rising star in the agitprop office of the Soviets as well as teaching at the Humboldt University. See Wolfgang Harich, "Ernst Jünger und der Frieden," *Der Aufbau* 1 (1946): 556–75.

had observed of Jünger's writings a few years earlier, "they consistently delight me, however opposed I may be."[38] Hannah Arendt, too, was struck by the defiant quality of the works Jünger produced under the Third Reich, noting that his diaries of the war years "offer perhaps the best and most honest evidence of the tremendous difficulties the individual encounters in keeping himself and his standards of truth and morality intact in a world where truth and morality have lost all visible expression." The example of Ernst Jünger, Arendt concluded, proved "that the somewhat old-fashioned notion of honor... was quite sufficient for individual resistance."[39]

Another admirer from the left-liberal spectrum of German letters was the writer Alfred Andersch. One of the founders of the Gruppe 47, Andersch helped create *Der Ruf*, one of the first important literary journals as Germany lay still in ruins, which called for advancing democracy and a revival of liberal German culture. A good example of his engagement on Jünger's behalf was a widely discussed speech given in 1973 to the literary elite at Amriswil, a small town in Switzerland known for its annual gathering of the most important writers in the German-speaking world. In his keynote address, Andersch celebrated Jünger as an ultra-modern author who, he argued, had anticipated the insights of Marshall McLuhan in his writings on technology and the end of the bourgeois era. Andersch argued that Jünger's position during the Weimar era was equidistant from the Nazis and the Communists, and that the tragedy of the Third Reich was that neither the heirs to the radical legacy of the French Revolution nor the conservative reaction to the revolution were able to close ranks and defeat National Socialism before it came to power. Andersch thought the left should learn to appreciate Jünger's radical critique of forms of technological domination in modern society.[40]

38. Quoted in Kiesel, *Ernst Jünger*, pp. 16–17.

39. Hannah Arendt, "The Aftermath of Nazi Rule," in *Essays in Understanding: 1930–1954* (New York: Schocken, 1994), p. 260.

40. On Andersch, see Neaman, *A Dubious Past*, pp. 96–98. Andersch's biography seems quite at odds with Jünger's. Born in Munich in 1914, he was active in Communist youth groups during the Weimar Republic and was interned for a short period in Dachau in 1933, where he was severely beaten. He subsequently retreated into the inner emigration and escaped the totalitarian state by traveling, often to Italy, and by reading and writing. When he read *On the Marble Cliffs* in 1939, he became convinced that

For a long time, breaking a lance for Jünger was viewed by the self-described anti-fascist left in Germany as a scandal. Any critic who seemed even slightly favorably disposed to the author of *Storm of Steel* became suspect of fascist, militaristic leanings. But Nemoianu overstates matters in suggesting that such polemics continue to rage today. With the passage of time, and following Jünger's death in February 1998, the battle positions have softened considerably. Indeed, the past fifteen years have witnessed something of a Jünger renaissance in Germany. His life and works are well-represented in seminar rooms and symposia and museums—the German Literary Archive in Marbach, sometimes dubbed "the Pantheon of German Literature," staged a massive exhibit of Jüngeriana in November 2010—and official recognition of Jünger, once the darling of Helmuth Kohl and François Mitterand, remains as strong as ever. When the Ernst Jünger Haus was recently reopened following renovations, the former president of Baden-Württemberg, Erwin Teufel, was on hand to deliver the commemorative address.

And what of Jünger's reception "in Anglo-Saxon lands"? Despite the existence of several of Jünger's later works in English translation—*The Glass Bees* (1957), *Eumeswil* (1977), *Aladdin's Problem* (1983), and *A Dangerous Encounter* (1985)—his reputation among Anglophone readers is still almost entirely a product of *Storm of Steel*. Jünger's famed chronicle of his forty-four months on the Western Front is, in fact, so unlike the decidedly anti-war view of the conflict familiar from the poetry of Wilfred Owen or Siegfried Sassoon that its lack of disillusion and high-minded disgust in surveying the carnage can too easily suggest a lack of humanity on the part of its author.[41] Peter Gay's summary judgment of Jünger's war writings as a "nihilistic celebration of action and

the book was a clear damnation of Hitler and the concentration camps. He nevertheless returned to Germany as the war began, but as the tide turned against Germany in 1944, Andersch deserted from the Army, something Jünger of course would never have considered. Andersch was, however, like Jünger in that he always acted independently, finding himself at odds with other members of the Gruppe 47 for their explicit denunciation of Jünger and Gottfried Benn. He found their refusal to hold readings or discussions of Jünger's and Benn's works distasteful and narrow-minded.

41. This is true even of the much-revised—and rather less bloodthirsty—1961 edition on which Michael Hofmann's excellent new translation is based. See Ernst Jünger, *Storm of Steel*, trans. Michael Hofmann (New York: Penguin, 2004).

death"[42] has been typical, even if scholars willing to take the case to trial have generally arrived at a more balanced assessment. (Helmuth Kiesel, perhaps the foremost student of Jünger in Germany today, argues that what appears to be a voyeur's delight in the display of corpses is better read as an "unsparing analysis" of war in the technological age, in which "nothing is sugarcoated or trivialized, and nothing is suppressed."[43]) On the whole, the modest stirring of interest in Ernst Jünger in the English-speaking world in recent years has rarely strayed from the most well-worn categories in the Jünger literature. The focus, in other words, remains resolutely fixed on Jünger's early right-wing nationalist activism, on his role as an influential exegete of the "war experience" for Weimar's wannabe warriors and disaffected veterans, and on his jarring prophecies (with seeming endorsements) of a fusty bourgeois world about to be liquidated by the dynamic, depersonalizing forces of "total mobilization."

The appearance in English of the 1938 version of Jünger's *The Adventurous Heart*, along with his "Sicilian Letter to the Man in the Moon" (1930), is, it seems safe to say, far more likely to complicate these established judgments than to overturn them entirely. But before turning to these texts, which provide such a rich statement of Jünger's peculiar aims and motives, it is worth considering for a moment how Jünger has been appraised by some of the most eminent English-language critics to have addressed his work. A few brief snapshots may indicate something of the interpretive richness of his writings. They can also help us understand why reactions to Jünger's prose, whether positive or negative, have been so universally strong. More importantly, perhaps, they may suggest where a fuller reception of his works might lead should a Jünger revival on these shores—on a par with, say, the now decades-long rediscovery of Carl Schmitt, with its astonishing diversity of assessments (from fascist anti-Semite to valuable critic of the flaws of parliamentary democracy)—one day take place. It can only be hoped that the guardians of Jünger's writings in Germany will show a continued willingness to allow English translations of his more overt political writings and his diaries. In our opinion, an annotated translation of Jünger's

42. Peter Gay, *Weimar Culture: The Outsider and Insider* (New York and London: W. W. Norton, 2001), p. 81.

43. Kiesel, *Ernst Jünger*, pp. 195f.

monumental World War II diaries, *Strahlungen*, would contribute decisively to a more nuanced and balanced understanding of this complex author, whose life and works are not reducible to monolithic categories.

Probably the most influential and oft-cited study in English has been J. P. Stern's *Ernst Jünger*, first published in 1953. Though riddled with inaccuracies and necessarily outdated, Stern's slender book remains the quintessential response to Jünger's oeuvre from the standpoint of classical humanist values. While conceding the epochal significance of Jünger's writings, Stern detected in them a "defective sensibility," one whose pervasive effects could be discerned in every line from his undeniably prolific pen. For Stern, Jünger had been wholly fashioned by the Great War: "[its] atmosphere, its language, the scale of values it imposed upon him, the shock and the numbing of sensibility—all this remains firmly imprinted on his mind." Jünger's failing was not as an authentic reporter of the existential moment—his descriptions of combat, Stern acknowledged, were unparalleled—but in his inability to connect such moments to the entirety of a human life, whose less exalted experiences were thereby reduced "not merely to relative but to absolute insignificance." Such overinvestment in the ecstatic as a source of meaning resulted, Stern wrote, in "contempt... for all life that is lived on any other but the 'existential level.'" This contempt also meant that Jünger's gaze, when it alighted on something other than scenes of terror and violence, failed to respond to the "particular as such," conscripting it instead into "a total view... in which men, things, and nature are all equally involved." Ultimately, his "manner of seeing and expressing things" was determined, not "by each live experience as it arises," but "by precedent rationalisation"—Jünger would forever remain, Stern concluded, "*endormie dans la méthode*."[44]

A similar indictment was supplied by George Steiner in a perceptive 1970 essay for the Anglo-American cultural journal *Encounter*. Steiner, like Stern an émigré from Hitler's Europe, also judged war "the visionary core, the final touchstone of the entirety of Jünger's work." And Steiner too sensed in Jünger's corpus a profoundly felt response to the modern evacuation of meaning, a need for a "total view" if the specter of

44. J. P. Stern, *Ernst Jünger: A Writer of Our Time* (New Haven, CT: Yale UP, 1953), pp. 10, 25–26, 30, 39, 43.

nihilism was to be kept at bay. But Steiner went further in recognizing the importance to this project of Jünger's relationship to the natural world. Jünger, he noted,

> regards zoology and botany as a school for precise feeling; the eye of the beetle-hunter, of the collector of orchidaccae becomes as penetrating and scrupulous as that of a sniper. Having immersed himself in the wasteful destruction of men, Jünger finds a guarantor of reality in the tenacity and profusion of organic life. That low perennial herb *Convalaria majalis*, the lily of the valley, will blow cool and luminous when our concrete bunkers are dust.... Like Goethe, Jünger deems the classification of floral species to be a supreme metaphor of reason, of the secret concord between the image of order in the human soul and the realities of significant relations in nature.... Moreover, to recognise plants by their sporophylls, as Linnaeus did, is to "read" an alphabet or cypher of life more ancient, more universal than any human idiom. In the tendril of the vine, in the hieroglyphs on the wings of the tiger-moth, the logic of creation is writ deep. The classic artist is one who can make his individual speech or form similarly suggestive of a hidden unity, of a total design of truth.[45]

For Steiner, however, the gaze that can locate order and beauty in nature grew frightfully cold when turned to the human realm. Jünger's "terrible detachment," his "fastidious, quietly observant discipline of feeling," was epitomized in his description of a bloody March 1942 bombing of the Renault works, which Jünger observed from occupied Paris. Though Jünger himself notes that hundreds were killed, he nonetheless adds that, "seen from my quarter, the affair looked rather like stage-lighting in a shadow theater." Steiner ascribed this presumed failure of fury and sorrow to a "grave defect of consciousness, an atrophy at the vital center." "Jünger professes to have spent a lifetime in combat against nihilism," Steiner inveighed, "[yet] there is in his own outlook—physically and psychologically implicated in the violent fabric of history as his personal career has doubtless been—a profound nihilism. Reading his work, one experiences what Emily Dickinson termed 'a zero at the bone.'"[46]

45. George Steiner, "The Zero at the Bone," *Encounter* 35 (July 1970): 72–73.
46. Ibid., p. 76.

Arguably the most sophisticated and intellectually satisfying treatment of Jünger in English is Marcus Bullock's 1992 *The Violent Eye*. Much of the value of Bullock's account, which took the two versions of *The Adventurous Heart* as emblematic of Jünger's maturation as a writer, consists in his helpful willingness to avoid mistaking the worst possible motives for the true ones. Though a root-and-branch opponent of virtually everything Jünger stands for, Bullock made no attempt to minimize the scale of Jünger's authorial achievement or his polymathic ability "to engage the full cultural heritage... on an equal footing." Indeed, Bullock approached Jünger with the seriousness more often reserved for studies of the Frankfurt School, whose positions, he observed, frequently "run parallel to Jünger's, though in opposite directions."[47]

The importance of Jünger's works, according to Bullock, lies in the genuinely independent, if "essentially alien," vision of human life they develop in reaction to the modern loss of a "continuity of experience" with the past. Supremely sensitive to what is at stake in the breakdown of tradition, and unwilling to embrace the substitutes offered by either fascism (a manipulative, ahistorical mythmaking) or liberal democracy (frivolous, present-oriented entertainment), Jünger's project became a lifelong effort "to construct the basis of 'universality' in his experience." Faced with modernity's "endless multiplicity of events," Jünger endeavored to supply, in other words, nothing less than an alternative foundation of reality able to ground their meaning and secure their accessibility to literary representation. "Much like Walter Benjamin," Bullock argued, Jünger "experiences history as a ruin. Unlike Benjamin, however, he looks to Being and the disclosure of nature to repair the loss." Jünger's "return to the physical immediacy of the senses" was a response to the absence of "permanence and continuity in the human domain. The classical image of mankind and the community of human experience in tradition are comforts he no longer finds valid amid the ruins of our violent world."[48]

Whereas other English-speaking commentators have found in Jünger's works a tired reiteration of anti-Enlightenment themes or a spiritual

47. Marcus Paul Bullock, *The Violent Eye: Ernst Jünger's Visions and Revisions on the European Right* (Detroit: Wayne State UP, 1992), pp. 15–18, 42.

48. Ibid., pp. 24–28, 33, 36–40.

aristocrat's snobbish disdain for mass society,[49] Bullock identified a project of urgent importance for the world of "established Anglo-Saxon values and truths." The presumed naturalness of these values, Bullock contended, means they

> must always be encircled by their own particular brightness of authority and stay beyond the light of critical scrutiny with which they themselves irradiate everything else. That is, the rationalist ideology produces a subconscious systematic limitation on its own critical rationality.... The relevance for the English-speaking reader of a figure like Jünger springs from the difference in his expectations from what is most natural to us, notably his skepticism about those bright ideals carried aloft on the bourgeois ship of state. While he may be quite wrong to regard them as bogus in themselves, he is nonetheless able to peer into the murky hold of the vessel without an insurmountable predisposition to find them carried as its sole freight.... As Jünger himself states, *any* perspective from outside the confines of a system disrupts the limitations of its boundary.

In Bullock's estimation, Jünger's works exhibit enough consistency and depth in their "irrational unfamiliarity" to provide an "imaginative Archimedean point from which critical leverage may be generated to test the pieties of our own tradition." Yet where Jünger's project ultimately fails is in its irrepressible need to magically transform objects and situations into "sources of rapturous symbolic presence"—"a lonely labor," he maintained, that never identifies "with human lives through the common bonds of individual needs, interests, and desires"—as well as in the feckless nostalgia of Jünger's longing for an irretrievably lost pre-industrial order.[50]

If Bullock presented a defense of Jünger from the left, Virgil Nemoianu, whose bemusement at the patterns of Jünger's reception we have already noted, offered a vindication from the right in a lengthy 2010 essay on Jünger's relevance to the postmodern condition—probably the most serious attempt yet made in the English-speaking world at a conservative appropriation of his oeuvre. For Nemoianu, the value of

49. For a succinct and representative case, see Ian Buruma's "The Anarch at Twilight," *The New York Review of Books*, June 24, 1993.

50. Bullock, *The Violent Eye*, pp. 30–33, 170–76.

Jünger's mature writings—heralded, as he pointed out, by the 1938 edition of *The Adventurous Heart*—lies in the tension they enact "between nostalgic traditionalism, on the one hand, and precise and mostly unbiased attention to change in all its details and implications, on the other." Amidst "the labyrinthine possibilities of an overinformed and subaxiological age," Nemoianu argued, Jünger was among those who still held out the possibility of "preserving for the future some memory, some subtle essence of the past... at the end of all our ephemeral turbulences and battles." This will to transmission was on the grandest possible scale. "[F]rom the 1930s on," he wrote, "Jünger was bent on extending the realm of cultural inheritance so it would comprise natural history (geology, insect habitats, botanical shapes, and colors), deliberately placing himself in the tradition of Buffon, Goethe, Bernardin de Saint-Pierre, Chateaubriand, and perhaps even Thoreau; he shared with this tradition the view that the structures of the biological realm should be read in (almost) cultural-historical terms." Jünger's expeditions into strange worlds—his exploration of dreams, his experimentation with drugs, his lifelong dedication to entomology—should be understood, Nemoianu suggested, as aspects of Jünger's intellectual and spiritual cosmopolitanism, his perennial alienation from the local, the present-bound, the normal.[51]

Far from the rarefied musings of an aloof aesthete, Jünger's sprawling interests combined into a "human" project of the first order. His cold "gaze," Nemoianu noted, is better understood as the defense of a "rich and sometimes painful interiority," the product of a "stoicism that protects and armors sensibility, nostalgia, suffering, and anxiety in the face of the waves after waves of an overwhelming future." Deeply affected by a full century of unprecedented destruction, Jünger's writings came to embody a "relentless search for a humanized science" and an emphasis on "the integrity and dignity of the human body and human soul." Indeed, according to Nemoianu, Jünger represents something of a guidepost for a "renewed" humanism altogether: "He is an important witness when it comes to the struggles and dilemmas that are now as important to the so-called third world as they used to be to some European areas fifty or a hundred years ago.... Jünger's writings constantly hark back to

51. Nemoianu, *Postmodernism and Cultural Identities*, pp. 285, 289, 294–96, 312, 318.

the pangs and the demise of the premodern world, and in his writings are recorded angry disorientation, impulsive rejections, an outreach toward stable and traditional wisdoms, [and] agonized doubts about rationalist technology."[52]

Whether and to what extent the shoe sized up for Ernst Jünger by these critics ultimately fits can be left to readers to decide. Certainly evidence abounds in the two texts printed here to support all of these contentions, and a good many besides. What's more certain is that these works are the indispensable entry point to the problems and perspectives of Jünger's later writings as a whole. These include his gradual development of the figure of the "anarch"—the inwardly sovereign individual most fully developed in *Eumeswil* but adumbrated here in the notion of "désinvolture"—as well as Jünger's ever-expanding concern to sort out a view of man's place in the world that extends well beyond the historical realm to a planetary and even cosmic scale. In a 1942 letter, Jünger himself described the 1938 edition of *The Adventurous Heart* as part of his "New Testament," in contrast to his fiery "Old Testament" writings on the First World War and his repeated paeans to modern technology and "total mobilization." As a transitional text, Jünger named his 1930 "Sicilian Letter to the Man in the Moon"—hence its inclusion in the present volume. But as with Scripture, so here too we are dealing not with a wholly new departure but with historically related outlooks; Jünger's "New Testament" thus reflects a maturation and a ripening of perspective, further construction from a "foundation" (Jünger's own metaphor) he preferred to leave intact.[53] It is hoped that the availability of these works in English will, at a minimum, contribute to what Nemoianu identified as a still-missing account of "the organic evolution of Jünger from the passionate flightiness of his young years to full maturity."[54]

For now, let us conclude by considering these two works in greater detail. Neither, it must be said, wears its meaning on its face. A few words of assistance to the reader, a few avenues of possible interpretation, may prove helpful.

52. Ibid., pp. 289, 292–94, 373n5.

53. Schwilk, *Ernst Jünger: Leben und Werk*, p. 187. See also Schwilk's recent biography, *Ernst Jünger: Ein Jahrhundertleben* (Munich and Zurich: Piper, 2007), p. 443.

54. Nemoianu, *Postmodernism and Cultural Identities*, p. 375n19.

III

"What immediately strikes one about Jünger's style," Bullock aptly observed, "is the extreme concern with concrete and factual material on the one hand, which includes his scientific work as an entomologist as well as the observation of current events in his journals, together with a pronounced and consistent tendency to interpret these facts as evidence of a dimension of life that is more removed and more totally at variance with a generally accepted image of human reality than occurs in almost any other writer's work."[55] Less evident on a cursory reading, but no less important, is the extraordinary diversity of components from which this strange "dimension of life" appears to be constructed. The 1938 version of *The Adventurous Heart* contains erudite references to, among many others, Hesiod, Kleist, Darwin, Dostoyevsky, Pausanias, Rivarol, Burckhardt, Bernini, Francis Bacon, Dio Cassius, Barthold Brockes, Hieronymous Bosch, Laurence Sterne, Octave Mirbeau, and the Tibetan Book of the Dead, along with a host of more obscure figures, the nineteenth-century gastronome Baron von Vaerst, say, or the sixteenth-century demonologist Johann Weyer. Though major influences on Jünger can certainly be identified (about which more shortly), the sheer range of his reading and catholicity of his interests makes any attempt to reduce him to a single movement or camp a difficult enterprise. As Thomas Nevin dryly remarked, Jünger may regard himself "as 'a field marshall of ideas,' but he calls no philosophical system to attention."[56]

It is no accident that Jünger is liable to come across as a latter-day Paracelsus (whom he also mentions, not coincidentally) in an age more accustomed to genomes and high-energy physics. Though fully alert to the scientific and technological revolutions around him, Jünger's "optic" is self-consciously *altmodisch*. His preferred readings, and the array of references in his work, tend to predate his 1895 birth. At the most general level, we can say that Jünger is concerned with the recuperation of ways of seeing and relating to the world that were superseded by the "modern," as that term is understood in Michel Foucault's *The Order of Things* and E. J. Dijksterhuis's *The Mechanization of the World Picture*. Not unlike Heidegger and Nietzsche, who pined for the pre-Socratics,

55. Bullock, *The Violent Eye*, p. 24.
56. Nevin, *Ernst Jünger and Germany*, p. 4.

Jünger too meets the challenge of modernity by looking for something recoverable in the past. And indeed, like Foucault, who foresaw the eclipse of the modern episteme and the consequent "death of man," Jünger was deeply conscious of the modern as a passing moment, a cognitive horizon bound to one day yield in turn. Richard Herzinger, referring to Jünger, coined the phrase *Übermoderne* to denote this "deeper" alternative to the postmodern.[57]

One measure of Jünger's distance from the inherited common sense of English speakers today can be found in his clear aversion to any ontological distinction between nature and society. This was evident as early as 1920 in his choice of *Storm of Steel* as the title for his memoir of the Great War, as though the conflict were not a man-made event with comprehensible socioeconomic and political causes, but an uncontrollable force of nature.[58] In 1930, Jünger wrote that "the heroic spirit is opposed to seeking the image of war in a source that can be determined by human action,"[59] and we might add that Jünger's "adventurous heart" shows a similar disinclination in most other domains as well. As Bruno Latour pointed out, this rigorous "divide between the natural world and the social world" is "constitutional" of modernity; as soon as one establishes a common conceptual framework uniting both realms, "one ceases to be modern."[60] No doubt something of the unnerving "coldness" of Jünger's prose, to which George Steiner is such an eloquent witness, can be attributed to this distinctly unmodern turn of mind.

57. Richard Herzinger, "Werden wir alle Jünger?" *Kursbuch* 122 (December 1995): 93–117.

58. This oft-made point should be balanced by a recognition that the metaphor is also a bit of a commonplace. Eric Hobsbawm, whose historical consciousness is about as far from Jünger's as can be imagined, also likened the outbreak of war in 1914 to a thunderstorm. See his *The Age of Empire, 1875–1914* (London: Abacus, 2002), p. 326.

59. Ernst Jünger, "Total Mobilization," trans. Joel Golb and Richard Wolin, in *The Heidegger Controversy* (Cambridge, MA: MIT Press, 1933), p. 122 (translation slightly altered).

60. Bruno Latour, *We Have Never Been Modern*, trans. Catherine Porter (Cambridge, MA: Harvard UP, 1993), p. 13. Nemoianu also points out that while Jünger's loyalty "to a metaphysical or ontological level of existence is of course a kind of heresy for those devoted to the dogma of pure processuality," this belief "was never accepted as absolute truth in either the Western past... nor in any extra-European culture. Jünger may be right or wrong in not acquiescing to such widely shared convictions, but he is certainly not at all idiosyncratic in doing so" (Nemoianu, *Postmodernism and Cultural Identities*, p. 293).

The 1938 version of *The Adventurous Heart* contains numerous arresting equations of this sort. In "Beach Passages (2)," Jünger is reminded by the silent gnawing of caterpillars on an aspen leaf of the "words of consolation that Condés gave to the weeping Mazarin over the six thousand fallen at the Battle of Freiburg: 'Pah, a single night in Paris gives life to more people than this whole campaign has cost.'" Without skipping a beat, Jünger allows both to stand for "the double accounting of life"—the indissoluble connection, that is, between creation and destruction—whose acknowledgement is "a sign of a healthy life that does not shy away from a bloody incision."

Jünger is no less disinclined to follow the modern tendency to seek comprehension in contextualization. Again, *Storm of Steel* reveals this bent in full flower from the very start. The book begins with private Jünger disembarking at the front near Bazancourt in the war's early months and ends with lieutenant Jünger's receipt of the prestigious *pour le Mérite* while recovering from wounds in September 1918. Throughout, Jünger's focus is on the scenes directly before him. Just as the meaning of the war was not to be found in any larger view of culture and society, but rather through an intense scrutiny of events themselves, so Jünger's later works—and his diaries most of all—show a marked resistance to relating the object of investigation to its mundane historical environs. As Jünger puts it in "Historia in Nuce: The Wheel of Fortune," the aim is to sift historical events for

> that which is valid always and everywhere.... A limited number of figures hide behind the plethora of the recurring. History becomes like a garden here, in which the eye sees, for the first time side-by-side, the flowers and fruits that are brought forth in constantly varying climates time and again by the flow of time. The extraordinary pleasure aroused by involvement with [histories of this type] derives from our perceiving while in a stationary condition that which only otherwise emerges in motion.

This "extraordinary pleasure" is by no means limited to such metahistorical musings. The exhilaration of such moments can be realized by lifting any object of investigation out of the normal "flow of time." In "Stereoscopic Pleasure," Jünger describes this as the "dizziness" we feel when "we enjoy the full depths of a sensory impression." His method here bears a striking resemblance to what Frederic Jameson identified as the "euphoria" of the postmodern reduction of experience to "pure material signifiers": "[The] breakdown of temporality suddenly releases this present of time from all the activities and intentionalities that might focus it and make it a space of praxis; thereby isolated, the present suddenly engulfs the subject with undescribable vividness."[61] That such anti-historicism translates, in Jünger's case, to a deep skepticism about "progress" or designs for stability and security on the historical plane is unsurprising.

In fact, Jünger has been identified as one of the main exponents of post-history, an understanding of the historical process that surfaced as an intellectual fashion in the aftermath of World War II. The idea of the post-historical condition was first developed by the French philosopher and mathematician Antoine Augustin Cournot, who distinguished between prehistorical, historical, and post-historical societies.[62] Cournot used the term *posthistoire* in the 1860s to refer to modern civilization transformed by scientific rationality, but it was his student Bouglé who coined the phrase. Hendrick de Man referred to Cournot in his book *Vermassung und Kulturverfall* (1951), and thereby introduced the concept to German intellectuals. Lutz Niethammer traces Jünger's interest in the idea to a revival in the 1930s of Hegelianism on the left and on the right, the former represented by the Alexander Kojève's lectures on Hegel's phenomenology, and the latter by Jünger's 1932 book *The Worker*. Both critiques attempted to undermine the rationalism of liberal humanism by adopting Hegel's definition of reason as the cumulative historical outcome of struggle and violence.

Common to both interpretations of history is the idea that political and scientific modernization has violently transformed all world cultures so that each loses its specificity and becomes part of a universal, planetary system. Both Kojève and Jünger use the term pejoratively, to castigate a bourgeois society that transforms human beings into mechanized, termite-like machine-animals. For the right, especially Jünger,

61. Frederic Jameson, *Postmodernism, or, The Cultural Logic of Late Capitalism* (Durham, NC: Duke UP, 1991), pp. 27–28. Jameson notes, however, that "anxiety and loss of reality" are as likely in such circumstances as any "intoxicatory" effect. For Bullock's own gloss on this aspect of Jünger's writing, see especially *The Violent Eye*, pp. 64–65.

62. See Lutz Niethammer, *Posthistoire: Ist die Geschichte zu Ende?* (Hamburg: Rowohlt, 1989).

Heidegger, Arnold Gehlen, and Carl Schmitt, in various versions of the same idea, the *posthistoire* world was characterized by the decline of Europe as a world power and the rise of purely technocratic societies, like the Soviet Union and America, to world dominance. For Schmitt and Jünger, the new imperial drive for hegemony was reaching into space, following the model of British global colonization of the sea. As a result, ancient cultures were now doomed. The "system" had come to dominate human history, as technology unified the world and eliminated all difference. The end of history implies that after the demise of Europe, intellectuals can only take stock of what has been handed down or lies in fragments. Nothing significantly new will appear. Eclecticism in fine art, architecture, and literature will prevail. Jünger captured this mood in the 1949 preface to the war journals where he observed that the Copernican quest for ordering the cosmos, and the diary as a modern literary form, fall together chronologically. They have in common "the bifurcation of mind from the object, the author from the world."[63]

Jünger's oracular style, his preference for noetic assertions over reasoned arguments, so evident here, follows from his peculiar way of observing the world around him. Nemoianu likened Jünger's manner of observation to Goethe's dictum that our aim should be "to contemplate with a quiet and finely observant eye."[64] Jünger himself, in an interview just before his death, acknowledged having been "punished with a precise power of observation," one that brought "far more objectionable things than agreeable ones" to his attention.[65] Whatever the object of Jünger's gaze, it is clear that his descriptions are made to carry a tremendous burden of meaning. As J. P. Stern wrote in a later essay, the 1938 version of *The Adventurous Heart* "offers a striking parallel with the work of Husserl and the early Heidegger.... The phenomenological method they develop aims at presenting the typical, trans-personal aspects of human conduct, mostly in familiar situations. What Jünger's capriccios record are parts of the phenomenal world (which Husserl calls the *Lebenswelt*), culled and transfixed in moments of intense observation."[66]

63. Jünger, *Strahlungen I*, p. 10.

64. Nemoianu, *Postmodernism and Cultural Identities*, p. 293.

65. Björn Cederberg, "Letzte Gespräche mit Ernst Jünger 1996/97," *Sinn und Form* 56 (September/October 2004): 658.

66. J. P. Stern, "Representations of the Self, Singular and Collective, from Kleist to Ernst Jünger," *Comparative Criticism* 12 (1990): 19.

Already in the 1929 version, Jünger had pronounced his own "fundamental experience" to be that "typical of my generation," holding that his consciousness could thus "be called upon by everyone in its most valid and unconditional sense."[67] The exemplary character Jünger claims for his experience and the universality he attempts to derive from it are on full display in the 1938 version's concluding piece, "The Fishmonger," which records an afternoon stroll in the Azores.

> The streets lay quiet in the midday light; I heard only a gay, frequently repeated call in the distance, and I was taken by the whim to follow it. I soon came upon a tattered fellow carrying a load of already stiffened fish up and down the narrow, lifeless streets that hardly a dragon tree or araucaria lent their shadow to. I followed closely behind him, without him noticing, and his wonderfully vocalic call enchanted me. He shouted out an unknown Portuguese word—perhaps the name of the fish he was carrying. However, it seemed to me that he very quietly added something else; I therefore drew so close behind him that I was like his shadow.
>
> Indeed, I now heard that as he ended his resounding call, he whisperingly muttered something else—a hungry prayer, or a weary curse? For no one stepped out of the houses and no windows opened.
>
> We plodded on like this a long while through the hot alleys, offering fish that no one wanted at midday. And I listened a long while to his two voices, the loud and resonant, exuberantly soliciting call, and the quietly despairing soliloquy. I followed him like an avid eavesdropper, because I sensed that this was no longer about fish but rather that I was hearing the melody of man on this lost island—his simultaneously strutting and softly imploring tune.

What is missing from this description of the world is the familiar vantage point of the autonomous, sensitive, desiring individual subject, a quaint throwback to an earlier era that Jünger no longer deems credible in the technological landscapes of the twentieth century. In its place, he offers a detached view, eavesdropping on life, to be sure, but without the customary emotional or moral commitments that might jeopardize the knowledge obtained from such a distance. This is clearest in Jünger's "Sicilian Letter to the Man in the Moon," in which he identifies with the eponymous lunar observer, from whose perspective patterns

67. Jünger, *Das abenteuerliche Herz* (Erste Fassung), pp. 33–34.

and structures can be discerned in the apparent chaos of earthly events. "[R]arely is it permitted us down here to see purpose fused with meaning," Jünger writes. "And yet our highest aspiration must be the stereoscopic glance that grasps things in their more secret and dormant physicality."

The search for this vantage point—whose telescopic distance, somewhat paradoxically, grants a "stereoscopic" awareness of additional dimensions of sense or value in the object observed—is the core of Jünger's epistemology. The surface of a phenomenon, to which our commonplace understanding has remained restricted, is rendered transparent, thereby extending our perception of it to include a range of magical or esoteric meanings. In the "Sicilian Letter," Jünger relates a moment of heightened awareness during a hike on the Monte Gallo near Palermo. What he knows to be a lunar terrain etched by valleys and cliffs is suddenly transformed by the "magical trigonometry" of an imagination capable of discerning a human face.

> [W]hat was unprecedented for me in this moment was to see these two masks of one and the same Being melt inseparably into each other. Because here, for the first time, a tormenting dichotomy resolved itself for me, which I, as great-grandson of an idealistic, grandson of a romantic, and son of a materialistic generation, had until then held to be irresolvable. It was not that an Either/Or changed into a Both/And. No, the real is just as magical as the magical is real.

It is important to recognize here that Jünger does not privilege the depths over the surface, the magical over the real, but rather insists on their simultaneous perception and equal validity. As he writes in "On Crystallography," one of numerous methodological pieces scattered throughout the 1938 version of *The Adventurous Heart*:

> It often appears to us that the purpose of the depths is to generate the surface, that rainbow-colored skin of the world whose sight so intensely moves us. In other moments, this colorful pattern appears to be composed only of signs and letters by which the depths speak to us of their secrets. Consequently, whether we live within or without, we are gripped by the anguish of one who is always turning away from wonderful riches in whichever direction he goes.

The crystal, "in which the depths and the surfaces are simultaneously clear to the eye," is in fact one of the master metaphors for Jünger's manner of reading the world. His self-imposed task as a writer is to reveal things "not... in isolation, not impulsively or randomly," but in their hidden relations, their enduring and coherent significance. Hence the often unsettling absence in Jünger's mature prose of all that is bounded by the ego and is thus of merely personal concern.

To point out that this hermeneutic project bears little similarity to the humanitarianism of an Albert Schweitzer is, of course, fair enough; but to suggest, with Steiner, that it constitutes an "atrophy at the vital center" is a separate charge altogether, one which, at the very least, too hastily collapses the method into the man. There is, in any case, no shortage of testimonies to the power of Jünger's "optic." Hans-George Gadamer, for one, deemed Jünger's "physiognomic vision on a par with conceptual analysis as a mode of knowledge."[68] Alfred Weber, brother to Max Weber and an influential theorist in his own right, found in the 1938 version of *The Adventurous Heart* a "deep transparency," one that enabled "pronouncements on otherwise inaccessible layers of reality."[69] In a series of interviews given in the early 1990s, the East German dramatist Heiner Müller indulged in metahistorical speculations clearly inspired by the kinds of observations made in Jünger's diaries.[70] He had to perform a balancing act, at least according to Wolf Biermann, between the demands of authoritarian socialism and his own apocalyptic imagination.[71] In any case, Müller praised Jünger's "cold gaze" for its ability to "much more precisely view" the social and natural worlds.[72]

Much else could be said of the "strangeness," especially for Anglophone readers, of Jünger's essentially aesthetic response to what he regarded as the deteriorating norms and values of a liberal, rationalist, technological modernity. Certainly his transgression against what he calls the modern "idiocy" with respect to death (see "At the Customs

68. Hans-Georg Gadamer to Ernst Jünger, June 1, 1973, A: Ernst Jünger, DLAM. See also Gadamer's *Truth and Method*, trans. Joel Weinsheimer and Donald G. Marshall (London and New York: Continuum, 2004), p. 530.

69. Alfred Weber to Ernst Jünger, November 24, 1937, D: Merkur, DLAM.

70. See Heiner Müller, *Krieg ohne Schlacht: Leben in zwei Diktaturen* (Cologne: Kiepenheuer & Witsch, 1994), pp. 275–81.

71. Wolf Biermann, "Die Müller-Maschine," *Der Spiegel*, January 8, 1996, p. 159.

72. Heiner Müller, *Werke*, ed. Frank Hörnigk (Frankfurt am Main: Suhrkamp, 2008), 12:555.

Station") can be counted here. Indeed, Jünger thought his accepting and curious attitude toward death the deep source of his critics' unease. As he wrote in 1988: "Politics is merely the provocation, my relationship toward death the actual reason. To some it has a stimulating effect, to many it is infuriating."[73] We might also include Jünger's evident lack of enthusiasm for extended narrative coherence. The diary form—composed, like broken glass, of sharply hewn fragments of observation—is Jünger's true métier. In his preface to *Strahlungen*, Jünger attributes this to the "speed" of modern life: "Perception, the multiplicity of tones, can escalate to such a degree that form is threatened.... [In such conditions] the diary is the best literary medium. In the totalitarian state, it is also the final refuge of communication."[74] Jünger wrote about photography in the 1920s and was intrigued by film. Some observers have even sensed an incorporation into the diary style of the modern aesthetic of rupture and montage associated with cinematography.[75]

Perhaps the best measure of Jünger's foreignness, however, can be taken from the three figures he considered late in life to have been the principal "stimulators" or "arousers" of his disposition:

> Rimbaud as a writer [*Dichter*]
> Schopenhauer as a thinker [*Denker*]
> Hamann as a magician [*Magier*][76]

We have already seen the debt of Jünger's stereoscopy to the "poetic synesthesia" of the French symbolist poets. Suffice it to add that Jünger derived from Rimbaud and Baudelaire (whom he might equally well have named) a conviction of the power of language to ferret out

73. Jünger, *Siebzig verweht IV*, August 12, 1988, in *Sämtliche Werke*, 21: 319–20.

74. Jünger, *Strahlungen I*, p. 13. Michael Hofmann puts it well in noting that Jünger's gifts "are primarily those of a diarist: descriptiveness and an ear for speech, attention to detail, mobility of perspective, intellectual stamina and disjunctiveness, at his best over medium distances, as a writer of passages rather than of books or sentences." See his "Introduction" to Jünger, *Storm of Steel*, p. x. We might also add that Jünger's novels (e.g., *Eumeswil*) likewise betray a predilection for disjuncture and internal monologues over external action.

75. See Norbert Staub, *Wagnis ohne Welt: Ernst Jüngers Schrift Das Abenteuerliche Herz und ihr Kontext* (Würzburg: Königshausen und Neumann, 2000). Staub cites Harro Segeberg's work on p. 15. For an elaboration on the film theme, see Harro Segeberg, ed., *Mediale Mobilmachung 1: Das dritte Reich und der Film* (Paderborn: Fink, 2004).

76. Jünger, *Siebzig verweht V*, December 14, 1995, in *Sämtliche Werke*, 22:209.

the perceptible world's hidden dimensions and unexpected correspondences, a belief in the "heart" as an organ of poetic perception, and a feel for beauty's ability to survive within depravity and repugnance. Indeed, it is here, rather than in any direct influence by contemporary French surrealists like Breton and Aragon, that the taproot of Jünger's aesthetic imagination is to be found.[77]

"The Tiger Lily," which provides an introduction to the 1938 version of *The Adventurous Heart*, suggests something of the deeper realities, or "figures," to which the language of Jünger's "capriccios"[78] aims to provide access:

> *Lilium tigrinum.* Deeply curved-back petals of a waxy cosmetic red, delicately but vividly speckled with numerous oval spots of a blackish blue. The spots are so distributed as to imply a gradual weakening of the life force that generates them. Thus they are altogether absent at the tips but so powerfully extruded near the calyx base that they appear to stand on high, fleshy, stilt-like outgrowths. Stamens of a narcotic tone of deep, red-brown velvet that has been ground into powder.
>
> The sight of it awakens an association with an Indian conjurer's tent, from within which a gentle prelude sounds.

The color symbolism here is significant. In "The Color Red," Jünger associates red with the primordial and dynamic forces of life; as the color of "fire, sex, and blood," it is "simultaneously menacing and enticing." In "The Color Blue," by contrast, we are told that blue suggests "remoteness" and "the elevated law-giving spirit." Whereas red is linked with urgency and unrest, blue evokes hesitation, spirituality, even "cheerfulness" (*Heiterkeit*). The specks of black on the tiger lily represent decay, decline, putrefaction, ultimately death. But black is also the color of soil and the earth itself, and as such a central symbol of being. The point is to think of flowers like the tiger lily as containing opposites inside of a unity. The flower evokes the image of a powerful animal, and is thus a magical circle of generative forces containing differentiation and unity.

77. See Kiesel, *Ernst Jünger*, pp. 153–55, 363–64.

78. According to Heimo Schwilk, Jünger takes the term, whose general meaning is a work of art combining real and imaginary features, from Francisco de Goya's *Los Caprichos*, a set of eighty socially critical and often dream-like aquatint prints produced in the late 1790s. See Schwilk, *Ernst Jünger: Ein Jahrhundertleben*, p. 371.

For Jünger, symbols are always at play in a force field of contractions, expansions, ambiguities, and paradoxes: life and death, pleasure and risk, totem and taboo, all transitory but enduring qualities of objects. Elsewhere, in a piece entitled "In the Greenhouses," Jünger again mentions the tiger lily, this time as a site of the interpenetration of "beauty and danger." The tiger lily thus stands at the beginning of *The Adventurous Heart* as a complex image: precisely described and "stereoscopically" extended, it alludes to the intermingling of form and tranquility with the formless and violent energies at the heart of life. The sight of the tiger lily brings forth the vision of an Indian magician's tent. The magician works stereoscopically: one eye to behold the external, the other the visionary and spiritual world. In a more Nietzschean register, the double level suggests—and beckons the reader to seek—the Apollonian consciousness that gives expression to darker Dionysian realities.[79] This example alone—the colors blue, red, and black are in fact found throughout these "capriccios"—conveys something of the intertextual intricacy of *The Adventurous Heart*.

The surface and the depth indicate the influence of Schopenhauer—the second of Jünger's great "stimulators"—albeit in this case via the young, eminently Schopenhauerian Nietzsche. *Heiterkeit*, which suggests a serene, even cheerful affirmation of existence, is undoubtedly the dominant attitude of *The Adventurous Heart*, if not of Jünger's mature work as a whole. Unfortunately, most of its resonances throughout the text have been unavoidably lost in translation. For Nietzsche in *The Birth of Tragedy*, the Apollonian qualities of "definiteness and clarity" were "the necessary result of gazing into the inner, terrible depths of nature.... Only in this sense may we believe that we have grasped the serious and significant concept of 'Greek serenity' [*Heiterkeit*]."[80] For Jünger, *Heiterkeit* is often invoked to express the fruits of stereoscopic perception, the crystallization in language of an image whose meticulous description simultaneously discloses some deeper vision. It also

79. "The Tiger Lily" has been repeatedly analyzed. See, for instance, Christoph Quarch, "Die Natur als inneres Erlebnis: Ernst Jünger's Perspektivenwechsel in der zweiten Fassung von 'Das abenteuerliche Herz,'" *Scheidewege* 23 (1994): esp. 301–3. See also Kiesel, *Ernst Jünger*, pp. 452–53.

80. Friedrich Nietzsche, *The Birth of Tragedy and Other Writings*, ed. Raymond Geuss and Roland Speirs, trans. Roland Speirs (Cambridge: Cambridge UP, 1999), p. 46.

names the pleasure in discovering that there is more to a phenomenon than first meets the eye. As he writes in "Flying Fish":

> Without success, but not without amusement, I was trying to catch some small, highly mobile, pearly-blue fish by reaching my hands into a bowl. When they could no longer slip away from me, they lifted themselves above the water's surface and fluttered gracefully around in the room by moving their tiny fins like wings. After tracing all manner of arcs through the air, they dived back into the water. There was something immensely heartening [*Erheiterndes*] about this switching of mediums.

This *Heiterkeit* is linked to a sense of inner security as well. In "The Combinatorial Inference," Jünger commends the glance able to take in "a whirl of multiplicity...with an even serenity [*Heiterkeit*]." More revealing is his praise, expressed in a 1937 letter, of the "god-like effects" found in "the secure *Heiterkeit* that reflects freedom from the fear of death."[81] Here Jünger clearly leaves behind the Nietzschean self-assertion of his earlier nationalist phase in favor of a more resigned posture, one akin to Nietzsche's "Greek serenity" and ultimately traceable to Schopenhauer's doctrine of aesthetic contemplation.[82] For Schopenhauer, tranquil contemplation of the dynamism at the heart of existence as revealed in music can quell the pain and anxiety which come from taking part in this very nature of things. Released from the striving of the individual will, one apprehends the metaphysical truth of the world as Will. Some intuition of this sort is doubtless behind Jünger's ability to take cheer from such seemingly cheerless spectacles as the sight (and smell) of decay on a beach. "Death here," he writes in "Beach Passages (1)," "is connected to the springs of life, and so its odor resembles a bitter elixir that drives off feverish fears." One detects similar Schopenhauerian residues throughout *The Adventurous Heart*, as for instance in Jünger's appreciation for the self-distancing that liberates us from a view of "ourselves as identical with blind will, with the formless life-force that fills us" ("The Redstart").

81. Ernst Jünger to Friedrich Georg Jünger, December 31, 1937, D: F. G. Jünger, DLAM.

82. Indeed, Jünger's lament in "On *Désinvolture*" that "our ideas of power have long been distorted by an exaggerated connection to will" seems an unmistakable reference to the late Nietzsche's "Will to Power."

The influence of Johann Georg Hamann on Jünger's strange reading of his experience is similarly profound and no less difficult to bring to the surface. Both versions of *The Adventurous Heart* carried as their epigraph a line from a 1787 letter that Hamann wrote to Friedrich Jacobi: "The seeds of my every consideration I find in everything around me." The context of the quote alone—Hamann is bemoaning the insufficient mastery of language that prevents him from fully expressing his meaning—reveals something of Jünger's purpose. In "The Gravel Pit," Jünger gives voice to a similar sentiment, noting that in picking up our own books, "we appear to ourselves as forgers in their regard. We were in Ali Baba's cave and have only brought a measly handful of silver back to the light of day." What Jünger calls for is a language able to express the "higher order of things," the forms or "figures" of a stereoscopically perceived reality. The task of language, he writes, "is to once more conjure up the waters that play with and around these forms—waters that at once stir and are *transparent*." This longing for an ur-language of deeper penetrative power is, of course, a foundational theme in Hamann's works. In *Aesthetica in Nuce*, Hamann proclaimed "poetry the mother tongue of the human race" and the poet the master of the sensuous images, metaphors, and analogies through which the author of creation had himself deigned to speak. One can hardly overstate Jünger's attraction to the idea, as he writes in the "Sicilian Letter," of a "language that aspires to the ultimate possibilities of understanding." Like Hamann, Jünger spurns the arid abstractions of the Enlightenment; such "great words," he proclaims, are no more real than "the coordinates that we lay over a map." Jünger turns his allegiance instead to "signs, metaphors, and keys of many kinds," to a "language of runes, which tells of a deeper brotherhood of being." In naming Hamann as a "magician," Jünger was acknowledging a debt to one who had taught him to see with the inner eye the harmonies in the world's apparent flux.[83] He was more explicit in a 1934 letter to Carl Schmitt. "I see in [Hamann's] view of Kant and the Encyclopedists," Jünger declared, "one of the most important encounters

83. See Bernhard Gajek, "Ernst Jünger's Hamann Erlebnis," in *Verwandtschaften, Jünger Studien* 2, ed. Günter Figal and Georg Knapp (2003), esp pp. 58–66. Cf. Walter Benjamin's own appropriation of this aspect of Hamann's thought in his "On Language as Such and on the Language of Man," in *Reflections: Essays, Aphorisms, Autobiographical Writings*, ed. Peter Demetz, trans. Edmund Jephcott (New York: Schocken, 1986), pp. 314–32.

between the eye and the ear, between light and language, between knowledge [*Erkenntnis*] and revelation generally. Since the Copernican revolution the inner and outer eye have fallen into opposition, and the concord between human and divine things has been replaced by the Cartesian pineal gland. But in this area there are still minds for whom the harmony has not been lost.... I count Pascal among this number, and language is for Hamann what mathematics is for Pascal."[84]

Let us conclude by briefly considering two important features of the 1938 version of *The Adventurous Heart* that may escape the reader. The first concerns the book's status as a work of the inner emigration. Though far less famous as an "oppositional" text than *On the Marble Cliffs* (published just a year later), the work displays an array of anti-Nazi gestures and images. These are at times quite subtle, as when Jünger observes that red in combination with black is especially "malevolent" ("The Color Red") or that it is "precisely the bad painter"—that is, the failed art student Hitler—who "unites with the mob" in driving beauty from the world "so that the ugly becomes passable" ("In the Museums"). Other pieces, presumably accounts of dreams, suggest the encroachment of terror into everyday life or appear to advance the bolder thesis that "progress" itself is always already implicated in barbarism. Thus, in "In the Utility Rooms," a nameless narrator stumbles through the back rooms and corridors of an elegant café in search of the toilet, encountering "red velvet" and "black cockroaches" along the way. He finds instead a room in which two patrons are being tortured. Making his way back to the dining hall, he now understands that the guests he had assumed were bored are in fact terrified. Perhaps the most arresting of these dream-like scenes is "Violet Endives," in which an opulent gourmet store where humans are found "hanging on the walls like hares in front of a game butcher's shop" is presented (with what degree of irony it is unclear) as a benchmark of civilization's advance. Several pieces, in fact, go so far as to describe postures of resistance. "The Elusion" lays out a "higher method of withdrawing from empirical circumstances." "Historia in Nuce: The Lost Position" comments on the isolation of individuals or communities in the midst of encroaching destruction, against which one can only prepare to die as a "sacral witness" to a better system

84. Ernst Jünger to Carl Schmitt, January 13, 1934, in *Ernst Jünger–Carl Schmitt: Briefe, 1930–1983*, ed. Helmuth Kiesel (Stuttgart: Klett-Cotta, 1999).

of values. "One particular figure of our destiny," Jünger writes, using a metaphor from no man's land, "may be characterized as that of the lost position." There are, to be sure, elegant and worthy thoughts here, and to publish them on the heels of Kristallnacht was, if nothing else, an act of moral courage. But these are not polemics against the Nazi state; still less are they calls to active resistance. Jünger had resolved, by January 1937, to "completely avoid political dialogue." As he set about assembling the pieces that would be published as the second version of *The Adventurous Heart*, he could do little more than build up the stoic defenses of his own "spiritual resistance."[85]

There is, however, perhaps one sense in which we can grant Jünger more than this. A second, by no means obvious feature of the 1938 version is the manner in which it continues, albeit in a more stealthy and subterranean fashion, the overtly radical project of re-enchantment that he inaugurated nine years earlier. Martin Heidegger, whose own reading of the political crisis of the early 1930s was decisively influenced by Jünger's writings,[86] characterized his "heroic realism" as a species of "romantic positivism." In doing so, Heidegger correctly recognized that what Jünger undoubtedly shared with the romantics—a longing for transcendence and wholeness, a concern for liminal zones and limit experiences—he also ultimately sought, not in escape to some land "where pepper grows," but in the reality that confronted him.[87] The "adventure" of the 1929 version was an attempt to locate this dimension of life in Weimar's urban and technological landscape. The book issued a call to a "hidden brotherhood" to emerge and join him in this revolutionary task.[88] No such vanguard appeared, of course. Yet the second version of *The Adventurous Heart*, though far less personal in tone, makes much the same appeal. Jünger still writes of "a longing for a fraternity without name" ("Solitary Sentinels") and of a spiritual elite able to "recognize

85. A lengthier reading of the second version of *The Adventurous Heart* in the context of the inner emigration, from which we have drawn here, can be found in Kiesel, *Ernst Jünger*, pp. 451–58.

86. See, for instance, Michael E. Zimmerman, *Heidegger's Confrontation with Modernity: Technology, Politics, and Art* (Bloomington and Indianapolis: Indiana UP, 1990), esp. chs. 4–6.

87. Martin Heidegger, *Gesamtausgabe*, vol. 90, *Zu Ernst Jünger*, ed. Peter Trawny (Frankfurt am Main: Klostermann, 2004), pp. 79, 90.

88. Jünger, *Das abenteuerliche Herz* (Erste Fassung), p. 175.

each other by secret signs" ("The Elusion"). Discussing his aims in a 1937 letter to Alfred Weber, Jünger made plain his expectation for "the formation of spiritual councils [*geistiger Gremien*], whose number one can imagine will be small enough. In saying this I don't mean that the nihilistic zone is already behind us. But it does appear to me that certain forces have overcome the zero point. We move past it either individually or in small bands." The more "outer insecurity" increased, he proclaimed, "the more confidence and inner *Heiterkeit* are stored up."[89]

What Jünger suggests here is that directly facing the condition of contemporary Germany, refusing to look away, as he did in *The Adventurous Heart* and for eight long years in *Strahlungen*, was intended as an act of community building (however small and diffuse) and as a gathering of spiritual capital for a post–National Socialist, even post-nihilistic, future. Already in 1938 Jünger had begun to adopt the role in which he would see himself after 1945, no longer a political agitator but a new Magus of the North. The "romantic positivism" mapped out in *The Adventurous Heart* would continue, however transformed, as a project to revolutionize everyday life by subjecting it to the "stereoscopic" enchantment of his own aesthetic imagination. Jünger and his circle would indeed constitute, in the Federal Republic, the "people of the day before yesterday and the day after tomorrow," not in the condescending and dismissive sense that phrase might suggest, but rather in the creative sense of a loyal but critical cultural and literary opposition to an Americanized, and increasingly global, modern and postmodern culture.[90]

~

By offering Anglophone readers this superb new translation of one of Jünger's most fascinating little books, we hope that this oft-maligned author can be viewed with fresh eyes. Even today, the German debates tend to be mired in extraneous ideological battles that overlay Jünger's

89. Ernst Jünger to Alfred Weber, December 14, 1937, D: Merkur, DLAM. As the correspondence makes clear, Jünger had sent Weber a pre-published draft of the work.

90. See Horst Seferens, *Leute von übermorgen und von vorgestern: Ernst Jünger's Ikonographie der Gegenaufklärung und die deutsche Rechte nach 1945* (Bodenheim: Philo, 1998). The overblown thesis of this book, which reflects much of the anti-Jünger hysteria on the German left, is that Jünger's writings actually contained a set of secret signals for the overthrow of German democracy and a revival of the German national revolution.

work with still onerous and poisonous residues about the Nazi past from inside the German historian's guild. Jünger's work and life are of course part of that contested past, a past that will probably never fully pass into history, but he is also too important to be reduced to a punching bag for those who just wish to settle ideological scores. We do not wish to make apologies for Jünger's politics. He was never a democrat and was less than enthusiastic about the new liberal Germany that Jürgen Habermas and other adherents of the German Basic Law promoted after 1949. He also published articles and treatises in the 1920s and early 1930s that were unmistakably hostile to Germany's doomed experiment with its first republic. He was hardly responsible for "burying" Weimar, but he certainly never lifted a finger to help save it either.[91] Non-Germans on this side of the pond, whatever their political proclivities and literary tastes, should be able to get beyond these facts and quarrels and examine with clear eyes the many other aspects of Ernst Jünger's life and works that assure he will have readers long after the dust has settled. We sincerely hope that this translation will be followed by many more, so that scholars and the general public will eventually have critical editions in English of the majority of Jünger's adventures in language and ideas.

91. In 1988, he wrote that in his view the German people are better suited to monarchy than democracy and that the Jews would have avoided persecution had the princes continued to rule. See Jünger's letter to Julien Hervier, a French editor of the Pléiade volumes of his war diaries, from October 23, 1988. Reprinted in Jünger, *Siebzig Verweht IV*, p. 328.

The Adventurous Heart

Figures and Capriccios

"The seeds of my every consideration I find in everything around me."
Johann Georg Hamann

"And so these things do all exist."
Ernst Jünger, *The Adventurous Heart*, first edition

The Tiger Lily **_Steglitz_**

Lilium tigrinum. Deeply curved-back petals of a waxy cosmetic red, delicately but vividly speckled with numerous oval spots of a blackish blue. The spots are so distributed as to imply a gradual weakening of the life force that generates them. Thus they are altogether absent at the tips but so powerfully extruded near the calyx base that they appear to stand on high, fleshy, stilt-like outgrowths. Stamens of a narcotic tone of deep, red-brown velvet that has been ground into powder.

The sight of it awakens an association with an Indian conjurer's tent, from within which a gentle prelude sounds.

Flying Fish **_Steglitz_**

Without success, but not without amusement, I was trying to catch some small, highly mobile, pearly-blue fish by reaching my hands into a bowl. When they could no longer slip away from me, they lifted themselves above the water's surface and fluttered gracefully around in the room by moving their tiny fins like wings. After tracing all manner of arcs through the air, they dived back into the water. There was something immensely heartening about this switching of mediums.

Flying Dreams **_Stralau_**

Flying dreams are like memories of the possession of a special spiritual power. In truth, they are more like floating dreams, during which a sense of gravity always remains. We glide forth into the twilight, close over the ground, and if we touch it the dream breaks off. We float down the stairs and out of the house and occasionally raise ourselves over low obstacles like fences and hedges. At these points, we push ourselves up with an exertion that we feel in our bent elbows and balled fists. The body is semi-prone, as though we were lying comfortably in an armchair, and we float with legs forward. These dreams are pleasurable; but there are other horrible ones in which the dreamer flies over the ground in a rigid posture, bent forward with his face down. He raises himself stiffly from his position, in a sort of catalepsy, by tracing a circle over his toes with his body. In this manner, he glides over nightly streets and squares, once in a while popping up like a fish before lonely passersby and staring into their terrified faces.

How effortless by contrast seems the lofty flight that we see on early floating pictures. Pompeii is a site for these kinds of finds too. A wonderful, uplifting vortex bears up the figures here, though it barely seems to ruffle their hair or robes.

The Gravel Pit **_Goslar_**

We so reluctantly pick up our own books again because we appear to ourselves as forgers in their regard. We were in Ali Baba's cave and have only brought a measly handful of silver back to the light of day. There is also a sense of returning to a state that we have since shed like a yellowed snakeskin.

This is what I am going through with these notes that I am opening again for the first time in almost ten years. I am told that for a long while now they have found their fifteen readers or so per quarter with astonishing regularity. A reception like this brings to mind certain flowers, like the *Silene noctiflora*, whose calyxes, while open a single hour one single night, are orbited by a tiny company of winged visitors.

Nevertheless, precisely this reconsideration of already concluded works has special value for an author—as a rare opportunity to grasp its language as a whole, to some extent with a sculptor's eye, and to work on it as a single corpus. In this manner, I hope to hit still a little more precisely on what may have captivated the reader. For a start, there should be no economizing on deletions; what is thereby saved can then be filled out from the reserves. A few forbidden pieces that I once put aside might also be appended—because when it comes to spicing a dish, we only gain a sure hand with the course of time.

As a figure for this diversity, I envision one of those depressions that we sometimes observe in dried-out streambeds during walks in the mountains. We find there rough chunks of stone, polished pebbles, gleaming flakes, and also sand—colorful debris that the whirling current brings down from higher elevations in spring and fall. Occasionally we take a piece into our hands and turn it back and forth before our eyes—a rock crystal perhaps, a broken snail shell whose inner spindle structure catches us by surprise, or a spike of stalagmite as pale as the moon, from an unidentified cave in which bats trace out circles in noiseless flight. This is the native soil of capriccios, of nocturnal larks that the spirit, as though from a lonely opera box and not without risk, takes a passive delight in. But there are also rounds of granite that have been polished in glacial mills, at points with sweeping outlooks from which the world appears a little smaller, but also clearer and more regular, like on copperplate maps—because the higher order of things is hidden in the manifold as in a picture puzzle. These are stupendous mysteries—with increasing distance we approach their solution. At the furthermost point, at infinity, they are comprehended.

Though there is thus no shortage of material, language should yet bring something more to it. Its task is to once more conjure up the waters that play with and around these forms—waters that at once stir and are *transparent*.

On Crystallography *Überlingen*

I seem to have learned a thing or two over the last years in regard to a literary device that illuminates the word and renders it transparent. Above all, I find it useful for resolving a dichotomy that often takes a powerful hold on us—the dichotomy that exists between the surface of life and its depths. It often appears to us that the purpose of the depths is to generate the surface, that rainbow-colored skin of the world whose sight so intensely moves us. In other moments, this colorful pattern appears to be composed only of signs and letters by which the depths speak to us of their secrets. Consequently, whether we live within or without, we are gripped by the anguish of one who is always turning away from wonderful riches in whichever direction he goes. Anxiety seizes us during the austere enjoyment of solitude, just as at the festively decorated table of the world.

A transparent structure is one in which the depths and the surfaces are simultaneously apparent to the eye. It can be studied in a crystal, which could be described as an entity able to both generate inner surfaces and turn its depths outward. I now pose the question if the world, large and small, is itself not also constructed on the pattern of the crystal—but in such a manner that our eye only seldom penetrates into this aspect of it? Certain signs suggest this is the case: everyone has at least once felt how people and things have been illuminated in certain significant moments, perhaps to such a degree that dizziness or even a shudder overcame them. This is true in the presence of death, but all significant powers, beauty for instance, elicit this effect—and we can ascribe it to truth in particular. An arbitrary example: the apprehension of the protoplant[1] is nothing other than the perception of its actual crystalline nature in a favorable moment. Our voices become transparent in the same way during discussions on matters that touch us to the core; we understand the other in a different and decisive sense, through and beyond the agreement in the words. In addition, it can be assumed that places exist where this kind of insight is not mediated by a state of exceptional elevation but where it belongs rather to the capital of a marvelous life.

In regard to the use of words in this sense, it is handy that language also possesses depths and surfaces. We have countless expressions at our disposal in which a plain meaning coexists with a deeply concealed one, and what is transparency to the eye is here secret consonance. There is also much in literary figures, particularly in similes, that bridges the deception of the opposites. Yet the process must be flexible—if we use a polished lens to observe the beauty of lower animals, we should not shy from threading a worm onto the hook in order to pursue the wonderful life living in the dark waters. It has always been required of an author that things not appear to him in isolation, not impulsively or

1. Goethe's *Urpflanze*.

randomly—the word is bestowed on him that it may be directed to the one and the all.

Violet Endives ***Steglitz***

Noticing a most particular kind of violet endive in the show window of an opulent gourmet shop, I went in. I was not surprised when the shopkeeper explained to me that the only meat that could be considered as an accompaniment to this dish was human flesh—I had already darkly suspected as much.

A long conversation ensued on the manner of its preparation, after which we descended into the cold rooms, where I saw the humans hanging on the walls like hares in front of a game butcher's shop. The shopkeeper pointed out that I was looking exclusively at hunted specimens and not those bred and fattened in captivity: "Leaner, but—I'm not saying this just to sell them—much more aromatic." The hands, feet, and heads were arranged in special bowls and had little price tags attached.

As we went back up the stairs, I remarked: "I didn't know that civilization had come so far in this city"—upon which the shopkeeper appeared taken aback for a second, but then took his leave with a most engaging smile.

In the Blind Quarter ***Überlingen***

All night I had been wandering around in the entertainment district of a large city, unaware of which country of the globe I found myself in. Some of the details recalled Moroccan bazaars, others fairgrounds like those found in the suburbs of Berlin. Around dawn, I landed up in some corner I had not previously noticed, even though it brimmed with life. Dance pavilions had been set up in the streets; ten, twenty, perhaps even more dancers were being shown off in front of each of them. As I watched, some of the passersby picked out a girl and took her into her pavilion to dance. I too joined in, though the girls did nothing for me since they were sloppily dressed and all had the same blank expression on their faces. And yet the moment they were touched, they grew more animated and warmed up. Being in the pavilion was not to my liking either; the music was too loud and the color scheme had been carelessly put together. The whole thing was a mystery to me, but when my eye passed over the carpet on which we danced, I guessed the solution.

It was fringed with round decorations, which were not however woven into it but rather stood up out of the close-cropped material like thin rounds of cork. I immediately understood that this was an inconspicuous measure to prevent the girls from dancing out beyond the carpet's edge—for these dancers were all blind.

As I left the pavilion, I sensed that I was hungry. A breakfast parlor stood directly across the street; inside, its proprietor received me with rolled-up sleeves. I ordered breakfast from him, and while he brewed my coffee and buttered my toast, he sent over a young man to chat. Only then did I realize that I had ended up in the blind quarter, because this young conversationalist had also been deprived of the light. The proprietor retained him as a sort of philosophical lure to attract guests to his tables. One proposed a theme to him, on which, as a consequence of his blindness, he would then take an unexpected and unusual position. But since he had no vision, his discourses simultaneously gave the guests a pleasing sense of superiority, which they tried to further increase by requiring him to speak on the theory of colors and similar things.

At that moment, I recalled that I had already heard this parlor mentioned as a favorite haunt of Berlin metaphysicians. The fate of the young man in this pub grieved me all the more in that I quickly recognized that he was capable of authentically profound and bold thoughts and that all he lacked was a little empiricism. And so in order to cheer him up, I thought up a theme so constituted that each of us, he as a blind person and I as a seeing one, could be superior to the other—for I did not want to humiliate him either through defeat or a cheap victory. And so we had a wonderful discussion over breakfast on "the unforeseen."

Terror — *Berlin*

There is a type of thin, broad sheet metal that is often used in small theaters to simulate thunder. I imagine a great many of these metal sheets, yet still thinner and more capable of a racket, stacked up like the pages of a book, one on top of another at regular intervals, not pressed together but kept apart by some unwieldy mechanism.

I lift you up onto the topmost sheet of this mighty pack of cards, and as the weight of your body touches it, it rips with a crack in two. You fall, and you land on the second sheet, which shatters also, with an even greater bang. Your plunge strikes the third, fourth, fifth sheet and so on, and with the acceleration of the fall the impacts chase each other closer and closer, like a drumbeat rising in rhythm and power. Ever more furious grows the plummet and its vortex, transforming into a mighty, rolling thunder that ultimately bursts the limits of consciousness.

Thus it is that terror ravishes man—terror, which is something altogether different from dread, fear, or anxiety. It is sooner related to the horror realized on the face of the Gorgon, with its hair on end and mouth opened in a scream, whereas dread more senses than sees the uncanny and for just that reason is shackled by it the more strongly. Anxiety lies yet distant from the limits and can maintain a dialogue with hope, while fright...yes, a fright is what is felt when the first sheet rips. In a deadly plunge, the screaming drumbeats and the glowing red lights then intensify, no longer in warning but as an appalling confirmation, all the way down to the terrifying.

Do you have any idea what goes on in this space that we will perhaps someday plunge through, the space that extends between the recognition of the downfall and the downfall itself?

The Stranger Visits ***Leipzig***

I was sleeping in an antiquated old house, when I was awoken by a series of strange sounds, which rang with a humming "dang, dang, dang" and at once agitated me in the highest degree. I leapt up and ran with a numbed head around a table. When I pulled on the tablecloth, it moved. There I realized: this is not a dream, you are awake. My fear increased, as the "dang, dang, dang" resounded ever faster and more menacingly. It issued from a vibrating warning panel hidden in the wall. Dashing to the window, I looked down into a narrow old alley that lay in the deep cleft between the houses, over which the ragged tail of a comet twinkled. A group of people, men with high, pointy hats, women and girls stood below, attired in an antiquated and disorderly manner. They appeared to have just run out of the houses into the alley; their voices echoed up to me. I heard the sentence: "The stranger is back in town."

When I turned around, there was someone sitting on my bed. I wanted to jump out of the window, but was spellbound to the spot. The figure rose slowly and stared at me. Its eyes glowed, and as their gaze intensified they grew in size, which lent them a horribly ominous aspect. At the instant their size and red blaze became intolerable, they burst and then trickled away in sparks, like bits of glowing coal falling through a grate. Only the black, burned-out eye sockets remained, as the absolute Void that lurks behind the last veil of horror.

Tristram Shandy ***Berlin***

During the skirmishes near Bapaume, I had *Tristram Shandy*[2] in a handy little volume in my map case, and it was still with me when we stood ready by Favreuil. Since we were kept waiting back at the artillery placements from morning until late afternoon, things soon got very boring, though our position was not without danger. So I began to turn its pages, and before long the entwined style, riddled with an assortment of lights, established itself as a secret accompanying voice in a chiaroscuro harmony with the outer circumstances. After having read a few chapters with many interruptions, we finally got the order to attack; I put the book away and by sunset I already lay wounded on the ground.

I picked up the thread again in the field hospital, as if all that lay between had been a dream or belonged to the content of the book itself, as the activation of some extraordinary mental power. I was given morphine, and I continued reading, at one moment awake, at the next in a half-twilight, so that a variety of different mental states chopped up and re-parceled the myriad layers of the text one more time. Fever attacks combated with Burgundy and codeine, artillery barrages, and bomb-droppings over our zone, through which a streaming retreat had already begun, during which we were sometimes completely forgotten—all this only increased the entanglements, so that today I am left with only a blurred memory of those days, of a half-sensitive, half-frenzied agitation in which even a volcanic eruption would not have astonished me, and during which poor old Yorick and honest Uncle Toby were the most trustworthy characters that presented themselves.

In these worthy circumstances, I entered the secret order of Shandeans, to which I have remained loyal to this day.

2. *The Life and Opinions of Tristram Shandy, Gentleman*, a novel by Laurence Sterne, originally published in installments between 1759 and 1767. Jünger is referring here to the fighting in late August 1918.

Solitary Sentinels ***Berlin***

Swedenborg condemned the "spiritual stinginess" that locked away his dreams and insights.

But what of the spirit's contempt for minting and issuing itself into general circulation, what of its aristocratic self-sufficiency in Ariosto's magical castles? The inexpressible is degraded when it expresses and makes itself communicable; it is like gold that must be mixed with copper to make it useful as currency. A dreamer, attempting to catch his dreams in the light of dawn, watches them slip away through the mesh of his thoughts, like a Neapolitan fishermen watching the fleeing silver shoals that occasionally stray up into the surface waters of the bay.

In the collections of the Leipzig Mineralogical Institute, I once observed a foot-high rock crystal won from the inner depths of the Sankt Gotthard during tunneling work—a most solitary and exclusive dream of matter.

Among the things that Nigromontanus taught me was the certain existence among us of a select group of men who have long withdrawn from the libraries and from the dust of the public arena, who are at work in the innermost spaces, in the obscurest of Tibets. He spoke of men who sit alone in nocturnal rooms, immobile as the rock through whose hollows that current flashes, which keeps all the mill-wheels and hordes of machines running in the outside world—but here it is liberated from all purpose and captured by hearts, which, as the hot, trembling cradles of all forces and powers, have withdrawn forever from the outer light.

At work? Are these the vital arteries in which the blood becomes visible under the skin? The weightiest dreams are dreamed on anonymous beds of soil, in zones from whose perspective work has something of an accidental character, a lesser degree of necessity. Michelangelo chiseled just the contours of the faces into the marble as his last step, then he left the raw blocks to slumber in grottoes like the cocoons of butterflies, whose inwardly enfolded life he entrusted to eternity. The prose of "Will to Power"—an uncleared battlefield of thought, the relic of a terrible, solitary accountability, a workshop full of keys, thrown down by someone with no time to unlock. Even someone in the zenith of his creativity, like Cavaliere Bernini, speaks of an aversion to the completed work, and Huysmans writes in a late introduction to *À Rebours* of the impossibility of reading one's own books. This too is a paradoxical image—like that of the owner of an original work who studies poor commentaries on it. The great, unfinished novels that were not completed because their very conception overwhelmed them—they resemble the construction of cathedrals.

At work? Where are those cloisters of the holy in which souls have won the treasure of grace in wondrous midnight triumphs, where are the hermits' towers that rise as monuments to higher companionships? And where has the awareness remained that thoughts and feelings are really immortal, that something like a secret double accounting exists, by which all expenditures rematerialize again as income in some very distant place? My only consoling memory in this regard is connected with moments from the war, when the sudden light of an explosion tore from the darkness the lonely figure of a sentinel who must have long been standing there. From these innumerable, dreadful night watches in the blackness, treasures have been accumulated that will only later be consumed.

Belief in these solitary men springs from a longing for a fraternity without name, for a deeper spiritual relationship than is possible between human beings.

Blue Vipers — ***Berlin, Osthafen***

I was walking along a monotonous, dusty road that passed through a hilly meadow landscape. All of a sudden a marvelous, steel-gray and thistle-blue patterned viper slithered past, and although I had the feeling that I should pick it up, I let it disappear into the thick grass. The event repeated itself, but with the snakes becoming increasingly dull, less attractive, and more colorless; the last ones even lay dead on the path, already quite covered in dust. Soon afterward I came across a pile of bank notes scattered in a puddle. I carefully picked each one up, cleaned off the muck, and tucked it into my pocket.

The Cloister Church — ***Leipzig***

We stood together in an old cloister church, cloaked in magnificent red and gold embroidered vestments. Among the monks gathered there were some, myself included, who used to meet at night in the burial crypt. We belonged to those who stray from the path because the beneficence of the powerful intoxicates them like wine. Our leader was a still young man, more richly dressed than all the rest. The soaring space, with its vaulted ceilings crisscrossed by colorful beams of light and its altars gleaming of stone and metal, held an oscillating tone within, like that which remains after the shattering of a beautiful, unused glass. It was very cold.

All at once our leader was seized and hauled up onto a choir bench. We watched as two golden candles that sputtered and diffused an anesthetizing smoke were held up to his face. Senseless, he was then dragged onto one of the altars. A group of minor brothers with faces of ossified malevolence surrounded the prone figure; but still colder than their glittering knives appeared to me the gazes of the hierarchs who emerged from the cloister at the high altar, at the sacristy portal and at the reliquarium, and observed the group in celebratory posture. The proceedings could not be seen; I only noticed with terror that the monks raised chalices to their lips, filled with a milky fluid on top of which there frothed a bloody foam.

Everything was consummated very quickly. The fearsome fellows stepped back, and the martyred figure rose slowly to his feet. We read in his face that he did not know what had happened to him. It had grown old, shrunken, bloodless, and as white as fired limestone. With his first step forward, he fell lifeless to the floor.

The warning, which conclusively reinstated the old order, filled us with tremendous fear. But, strangely enough, another sentiment mixed itself in with that razing pain whose memory has accompanied me since then like a second consciousness. I perceived it like a thump that wakes one up from sleep. As an abrupt shock sometimes lends speech to the mute, so the theological sense of things touched me from that moment on.

Conviction — *Berlin*

We must distinguish between merely knowing something and also being convinced of it. The difference between what is known and what is gained through conviction is like that between an adopted and a natural child. Conviction is a spiritual act that takes place in the dark—a secret suggesting and an innermost consenting, which is not subject to the will.

Accordingly, even the most conscientious studies do not take us beyond a certain definite intellectual rapprochement. Often, without realizing it, we continue these efforts once the lights are out. We not only learn in our sleep, we are also taught. But then we no longer grasp words, sentences, and conclusions, but rather a fantastical mosaic composed of figures. Thoughts appear in rhythmic whirls, and systems appear as architecture. We awaken with the sense that new channels have been laid in our inner landscape, or that we have been practicing with exotic weapons.

In this manner, we grasp the secret teachings that are concealed in every language of merit, that veil themselves with words. Only such messages possess convincing power; but the contact enriches us only if the fertile ground within us arches up to it.

The Master Key **Berlin**

Every meaningful phenomenon resembles a circle, whose periphery can be traced by day in fullest clarity. At night, however, the periphery disappears and the phosphorescent midpoint shines forth like the flowers of the little plant *Lunaria*, which Wierus talks about in his book *De Praestigiis Daemonum.*[3] In the light, the form appears, in the darkness, the procreative power.

Our understanding is such that it is able to engage from the circumference as well as at the midpoint. For the first case, we possess ant-like industriousness, for the second, the gift of intuition.

For the mind that comprehends the midpoint, knowledge of the circumference becomes secondary—just as individual room keys lose importance for someone with the master key of a house.

It is the mark of minds of the first order that they possess a master key. Like Paracelsus armed with the caper spurge,[4] they penetrate effortlessly into the single rooms, arousing the wrath of the specialists who watch their banks of files invalidated with a single stroke.

3. *De Praestigiis Daemonum* was a well-known work in demonology by Johann Weyer, also known as Wierus, first published in Basel in 1563. *Lunaria* is a genus of flowering plants in the family *Brassicaceae*. It includes two species with the common names "perennial honesty" and "annual honesty."

4. Caper spurge (*Euphorbia lathyris*) has been used for centuries in folk medicine as a poison, an antiseptic, and a purgative; it was a folk remedy for cancer, corns, and warts.

Our libraries thus bring to mind the geological worldview of Cuvier:[5] fossil deposits commemorating bustling activities, set down layer upon layer by catastrophic irruptions of genius. It also explains why fresh life entering these ossuaries of the human spirit feels the kind of fear that is awakened by the proximity of death.

The Combinatorial Inference — *Berlin*

Higher insight does not live in the separate compartments but in the structure of the world. It corresponds to a mode of thinking that does not move around in isolated and parceled-off truths but rather in meaningful connections, whose power to order lies in its combinatorial faculty.

The tremendous pleasure that comes from engaging with such minds resembles a walk through a landscape distinguished as much by the span of its boundaries as by the richness of its particulars. The viewpoints alternate in a whirl of multiplicity, yet all the while the glance takes them in with an even serenity, never losing itself in abstrusity and malformations or in pettiness and eccentricity. Despite the plethora of variations that the mind is able to generate and the ease with which it can switch fields, it perseveres with effortless rigor in making its connections. Its powers appear to grow as much when it turns from the motif to the execution, as when it returns from execution to motif. Using a variation on Clausewitz's fine image, we can compare this mode of movement with a walk through a convoluted garden in which we are able from every point to see the high obelisk erected at its center.

The combinatorial faculty differs from the merely logical one in that it proceeds with a continuous sense of the whole and never loses itself in singularities. Where it does touch on the individual instance, it is like a compass made of two different metals, whose gold point is seated at the center. In this manner, it is dependent to a far lesser degree on data; it disposes over a superior mathematics that understands how to multiply

5. Jean Léopold Nicolas Frédéric Cuvier (1769–1832), known as Georges Cuvier, a French naturalist and zoologist, as well as a major figure in natural sciences research in the early nineteenth century. He was instrumental in establishing the fields of comparative anatomy and paleontology through his work comparing living animals with fossils. He is well known for establishing extinction as a fact, being the most influential proponent of catastrophism in geology in the nineteenth century, opposing the evolutionary theories of Lamarck and Geoffroy Saint-Hilaire.

and exponentiate, while normal arithmetic has to make do with simple addition.

Hence, when a genius cares to enter the field of science, he engages in a brief, decisive clash with the specialists, who are basically only able to engage him in a straight line, while he can effortlessly outstrip and cut them down from the flanks. His preeminence emerges soonest and most brilliantly in the art of war.

To the extent that one of the intellect's tasks is to order things according to their relationships, the combinatorial inference shows its superiority by its mastery of the genealogy of things and its ability to trace their deep affinities. Simple inference in contrast finds itself limited to determining the superficial similarities and so breaks its back in measuring the leaves on the genealogical tree, while their fundamental dimensions in fact lie buried in the germinal cells of the roots.

Incidentally, an eminent specialist too may be recognized by his disposition over more comprehensive reserves than are comprised in his discipline. Every significant individual work has at least a drop of the combinatorial faculty mixed into it—and how inspired we feel when we stumble already in the introduction across those simultaneously powerful and playful sentences by which sovereignty shows its presence. This is a salt that withstands time and all its advances.

The Black Knight — *Leipzig*

I stand in a suit of black steel armor before a hellish castle. Its walls are black, the monstrous towers blood-red. White flames flare up like blazing columns before the gates. I trudge through, cross the castle's courtyard, and climb the stairs. Hall after hall, one after another, opens up before me. The ring of my footsteps reverberates on the stone-block walls, otherwise it is dead silent. At last I step into a circular tower room, above whose door a red snail has been chiseled into the stone. It is windowless, yet one senses the immense thickness of the walls; no light burns, yet a shadowless luster illuminates the space.

Two girls are sitting around a table, one black-haired, the other blonde, and also a woman. Though the three do not resemble each other, they must be mother and daughters. On the table in front of the black-haired girl lies a pile of long, glittering horseshoe nails. With great care, she takes them one after another into her hands, tests their points, and then stabs them into the blonde's face, limbs, and chest. The blonde does not move, utters not a sound. At one point, the black-haired girl brushes the other's skirt aside and I see that her thighs and lacerated abdomen are no more than a single bloody wound. A profound slowness clings to these noiseless movements, as if some hidden device is slowing down the flow of time.

The woman sitting across from these two also keeps quiet and still. Like in rustic pictures of saints, she wears a large heart cut out of red paper on her breast, which it almost entirely masks. With terror, I notice that with each nail thrust the blonde receives, this heart turns snow-white, like white-hot iron. I lurch toward the exit, with a sense of being inadequate to the test. Door after door flies by, each sealed with steel locks. There I realize: behind every one of these doors, from the deepest dungeon to the highest tower chamber, endless tortures are playing out, which no one will ever come to know of. I have penetrated into the secret castle of pain, but even its first model was too much for me.

Stereoscopic Pleasure — ***Berlin***

In the aquarium, at the coral fish. One of these creatures was superlatively colored, a deep dark-red, striped with velvety-black bands, of a hue only possible on this planet at those places where the flesh is produced in islands. Its creamy body seemed so thoroughly tender, so thoroughly color, that I felt I could push through it with a very gentle poke of my finger.

At this sight, I became aware of a pleasure of a higher grade, namely, the stereoscopic sensibility. The delight that a color like this awakens arises from a perception that embraces more than the sheer color. Something else takes part here, which we might call a tactile quality, a sensation in the skin that makes the thought of touching the object seem pleasant.

This tactile quality emerges above all in very light and very rich colors, but also in metallic ones, and painters accordingly know how to employ them to cross over into the domain of the sense of touch, as Titian does for instance in his garments and Rubens in his bodies, which Baudelaire called "cushions of fresh flesh."

This characteristic is integral to whole genres of paintings, such as the pastel; and it is no coincidence that pastel painting delights in taking the comely heads of women as subjects. It is one of the erotic arts, and there is something symbolic in the fact that its "velvet," the initial florid glaze of its colors, disappears so soon.

Stereoscopically, we especially enjoy carnation, foliage, streak, glaze, transparency, varnish, and ground,[6] say the grain on a wooden table, the fired clay of a vase, or the chalky porosity of a plastered wall.

To perceive stereoscopically is to simultaneously obtain two sense qualities from one and the same shade, and that with a single sense organ. This is only possible by one sense going beyond its proper abilities and taking on those of another sense. A red, fragrant carnation: this then is not a stereoscopic perception. But we can perceive a velvet-red carnation stereoscopically, as also the cinnamon smell of cloves,[7] in which not only is the smell affected by an aromatic quality, but the taste is simultaneously affected by a spice quality.

In this regard, visiting a laden table is also illuminating. The aromas of the seasonings, fruits, and fruit juices are not only smelled but also tasted; sometimes, for instance with Rhine wines, the aromas are even finely differentiated according to color. The encroachment of taste into the realm of the sense of touch is striking; it goes so far that in many dishes the enjoyment of the consistency is predominant, indeed, the actual taste recedes far into the background in some of them.

It can be no coincidence that this is particularly common in the most vaunted of things. One of these is Mousseux, which gives sparkling wine its special place among wines. Something else to be included here is the question of what is so special about oysters; until we consult our sense of touch, this can only remain unanswered. Here the sense of taste is forced to overstep its boundaries; and it is grateful to us for helping it out with a drop of lemon juice. In just the same manner, Eau de Cologne seems for many to be more of a refresher than a perfume; for this reason, we like to add a drop of musk to it.

6. *Carnation* (*Karnation*)—an old term describing the rosy pink, flesh color of a female portrait. *Glaze* (*Lasur*)—the laying of a transparent color over previously laid and dried-out pigments. *Varnish* (*Firnis*)—protective coatings for oil paintings, tempera, acrylic, alkyd, gouache, and watercolor. *Ground* (*Untergrund*)—a prepared surface on which painting is to be carried out.

7. The German word used by Jünger, *Nelke*, means both carnation and clove.

The Baron Vaerst[8] remarked in his *Gastrophie*[9] that precisely the objects that lie on the borders of the natural realm are especially tasty.[10] There is something correct in this, insofar as it nearly always involves extreme excursions to things that are in fact barely edible. Their finer, deeper allure depends on a more powerful orchestration of the sense of touch, and there are cases in which this stimulus almost entirely takes over from the role of taste.

Generally speaking, the sense of touch, from which all other senses derive, seems to plays a special role in perception. Just as we have to repeatedly fall back on intuition when our concepts leave us in the lurch, so we draw directly on the sense of touch for many of our perceptions. For this reason, we like brushing our fingertips over new, unusual, or precious things—this is as much the gesture of a naïve as of a cultivated character.

Returning to stereoscopy: its action consists in grasping things with our inner claws. The fact that this happens via a single sense that, as it were, splits itself greatly increases the subtlety of this grasp. True language, the language of poets, is distinguished through words and images that are seized in this manner, words, which although they are long familiar to us, unfold like flowers and appear to radiate an immaculate luster, a colorful music. It is the secret harmony of things that sounds here, of whose origins Angelus Silesius said:

> In the spirit the senses are one sense and one function all:
> The contemplator of God tastes, feels, smells, and hears him too.

Every stereoscopic perception causes dizziness in us, as we enjoy the full depths of a sensory impression that at first only presented us

8. Friedrich Christian Eugen Baron von Vaerst (1792–1855), known as Chevalier de Lelly, was a Prussian officer, later a writer and theater director in Breslau, and a gastronomist.

9. *Gastrosophie oder die Lehre von den Freuden der Tafel* (Leipzig: Avenarius & Mendelssohn, 1851).

10. Interestingly, the English *taste*, so similar in sound to the German *tasten* (to touch), derives from a thirteenth-century usage meaning "to touch, to handle," by way of the Old French *taster*, "to feel, touch," and the Vulgar Latin *tastare*, apparently an alteration of *taxtare*, a frequentative form of the Latin *taxare*, "to evaluate, handle." Incidentally, the ancient Greeks recognized eight tastes; in addition to the fundamental "sweet," "bitter," "acid," and "salt," they also had "rough, harsh" (*austeros*) and "oily, greasy" (*liparos*), that is, "tactile" tastes, in line with what Jünger describes here.

its surface. Between our astonishment and our delight there comes a shudder, like that from a thrilling plummet that simultaneously holds a secret confirmation—we feel the play of the senses gently moving, like a mysterious veil, like a curtain on the marvelous.

There is no dish on this table without at least a grain of the spice of eternity in it.

The Elusion ***Leipzig***

...and thus I was introduced to methodology by Nigromontanus,[11] an excellent teacher, whom I regrettably must grope to remember at all. That I almost completely forgot him lies in the fact that he loved erasing his tracks behind him, like an animal living in the deepest bush. Yet the comparison is ill-chosen; it would be better to speak of him as a ray of light that makes the hidden visible, while itself remaining invisible.

Only when I am in good spirits, enjoying an excellent inner barometer, do certain of his peculiarities return to me, but even then only like characters of a long-forgotten script. Thus I strive time and again without success to mentally retrace the way to his workshop, as someone might try to recall old paths to school. In pondering this, I get into a peculiar muddle. For instance, I know that he lived on the third floor of a Braunschweig apartment block that rose up between the trees near the Oker. There were rubbish dumps scattered through the district, their fences entwined with the tendrils of bittersweet nightshades; wild oats crept over the waste heaps and thorn apples shook their bells in the evening breeze. As I walked along the narrow paths, I would hear the thrushes, wrens, and gold chicks that accompanied me fluttering in

11. This figure recurs throughout Jünger's works, sometimes under the name "Schwarzenberg" or simply "the master" (*Magister*). Among the explanations that have been put forward are: (1) an allusion to the Leipzig philosopher Hugo Fischer, a close friend in the 1920s and 1930s, who introduced Jünger to the works of J. G. Hamann; (2) a reference to the character "Montan" in Goethe's *Wilhelm Meister*; (3) a transposition to the third person of ideas delivered in the first person in the 1929 version of *The Adventurous Heart*; (4) a self-portrait of the author more generally. These are not, needless to say, mutually exclusive possibilities. The figure also bears comparison with "Phares" in Jünger's *Heliopolis* and *Aladdin's Problem*. For the most extensive treatment of this crucial figure in Jünger's work, see Bernhard Gajek, "Magister—Nigromontan—Schwarzenberg: Ernst Jünger und Hugo Fischer," in *Revue de littérature comparée* 4 (1997): 479–500.

the hedges. Neither street lamps nor signs had yet been installed here, and so it often happened that I lost my way. In my memory, these mis-trodden routes become magnified in an inextricable manner, so that it almost seems he lived on an island in the middle of an archipelago, an island no ship could approach because the compass deviation confounded all calculations.

Now I remember that he once spoke of certain features of the Magnetic Mountain, of spiritual centers of such repellent power that they were unapproachable by ordinary senses and more unknown than the dark side of the moon. This was during his lecture on meta-logical figures, in particular on the one he denoted as the elusion. By elusion, he intended a higher method of withdrawing from empirical circumstances. He thus viewed the world as a hall with many doors that everyone uses and others that are only visible to a few. Just as otherwise strictly sealed castle doors are opened when princes make an appearance, so these invisible doors spring open before the spiritual power of higher man. They are like fissures in the coarse structure of the world, which only the subtlest powers are able to slip through; and all those who have ever passed through them recognize each other by secret signs.

Anyone knowing how to enter the elusion in this manner enjoys the marvelous calm of solitude in the center of huge cities and storms of activity. He penetrates into disguised chambers that are less subject to gravity and the assaults of time. Thinking is lighter here—in an incomprehensible instant, the mind harvests fruits it would not otherwise gather in years of work. The difference between present, past, and future also falls away. Judgments become as benevolent as a bright flame, unclouded by the influence of passion. Here a man also finds the right measure by which to assess himself when he stands at the crossroads.

Nigromontanus could tell us of solitary spirits, whose dwellings, though they seemed to be in our midst, were in an absolutely inaccessible world. Accustomed to the purest, highest grade of fire, they came forth only when the proximity of the highest danger made the transition tolerable for them. But he also felt that anyone who moves actively in an inverted orientation to the world and is capable of the elusion for just a moment should already be considered fortunate. As an analogy of such moments, he liked to mention the short silence following a demand to surrender—which is then refused.

As highly as he praised the power of crossing the walls of our dull senses, so he also took care to warn against that contempt for humanity, which the sight of the weak all too readily engenders. When touching on this subject, I often heard him allude to the one elusion that everyone, down to the last, is able to enter: as the most important of invisible gates, the gate of death was open day and night for us all, without exception. He called death the most wondrous voyage a man was capable of, a true work of magic, the cloak of invisibility par excellence, and also the most ironic rebuttal in the eternal dispute, the last, unassailable fortress of all free and brave men. In treating this material, he was quite inexhaustible with his metaphors and praises.

It is unfortunately true that I all too soon forgot his teachings. Rather than sticking with my studies, I entered the world of the Mauritanians,[12] those subaltern technicians of power.

In the Shops (1) ***Goslar***

Among the things I find remarkable in shops is the shopkeepers' stubborn tendency to specially wrap up even items that are themselves already perfectly packaged, a chocolate bar for example. Like all acts of courtesy, this practice has its background.

In the first place, we may certainly suspect a remnant of the ceremonies that trade was once associated with or even dependent on. This emerges even more clearly in open markets, where a festive kind of mood always prevails. Livestock trade in particular has its rituals, sacrifices, and incantations even today. The groups of haggling traders at horse markets carry on their commerce as in cyclopean times. Originally, the merchant must definitely have been the party in greater need of protection and therefore the one especially dependent on ceremonial affirmation, whereas the buyer all too readily transformed into a violent brigand. Phoenician relationships extend right into our own times; we encounter them again in reading the reports of South Sea travelers.

In every seller there lives a natural inclination to give a final, conclusive touch to the goods. Moreover, the covering, wrapping, and tying up

12. In Jünger's *On the Marble Cliffs* (1939), the "Mauritanians" are the Chief Ranger's army of toughs and vandals. His use of the term here seems a clear reference to the veterans' leagues and "conservative revolutionary" circles with which Jünger was affiliated during the Weimar period. The tone of regret in this passage also suggests an act of self-criticism.

of goods has a concealing aspect; the under-the-table transactions are the especially prized ones. In our times, an additional class-related character is present in practices like these, inasmuch as the great assault of technology on the world of the estates is extended also to the merchant class. In this sense, weighing, measuring out, and the various forms of packing are acts by which the merchant still partakes of that old state of affairs depicted in *Debit and Credit*[13] or *Behind the Counter.*[14] In this way, he defends himself from the encroachment of industry, which seeks to demote him to the level of a mere distributor. Yet zones already exist today where the battle has been decided against him. One of these is the tobacco shop. It can barely still be spoken of in the old sense as a shop; it is more of a kiosk. The dealing here has been pared down to a minimum; in a single grasp, the buyer has his goods in his hands, consigned to him as an always-identical, weighed, measured, and taxed little packet. An enormous expansion of this form of sale may be anticipated for the next decades, penetrating into areas no one today can even imagine.

But there are also places where we cannot lay any claim to packaging, in post offices and at train station counters for example. The quarrels to be observed here arise from the buyers' sense of the absence of the courteous conventions characteristic of commercial trade. The secret distinction operating here is that between clientele and public. In buying postcards in a shop, we form a very different relationship than if we bought the same cards at a public counter. The distinction is expressed even in the external arrangements. Merchants' shop counters are built as wide as possible, so that buyers can be served next to each other; access to public counters on the other hand is set up as a form of sequential processing. And while merchants invariably try to extol their wares, public clerks are always inclined to make objections, to divert us to other counters, to hand over only predefined quantities, and in general to repulse rather than attract the buyer. The difference becomes most apparent when large quantities are desired, in which case the merchant becomes amiable, the clerk on the other hand apprehensive. These are

13. Gustav Freytag (1816–1895), a nationalist German dramatist and novelist, who gained literary fame with the publication of his *Soll und Haben* (*Debit and Credit*) in 1855.

14. Friedrich Wilhelm Hackländer (1816–1877) wrote *Handel und Wandel* (*Behind the Counter*) in 1868, based on his unhappy apprenticeship in a store.

instructive advance skirmishes between the traders and the civil service, or between the casts of scribes and of merchants. The encounter attains grand dimensions when one of these deportments battles out a victory over the other, as is happening today for instance in the implementation of planned economies. In this case, as we could observe during the wars, the shops are all transformed into cashier halls, in front of which the public waits in long lines to be processed. The reverse development takes place when the merchants triumph; after losing the war, the cashier halls were adapted to the style of emporiums. Incidentally, wherever the merchants gain access to power on their own terms, a certain overlap occurs between these circles. High finance thus emulates governmental organization; we speak of bank clerks and bank counters, and the treasuries are built like fortresses.

Returning to the tobacco shops, I notice that many customers like to hang around in them a little longer than in other shops. The latest news, politics, and weather are discussed—one generally enters the shop with a pleasant feeling. In this respect, these businesses have a certain similarity with stand-up beer halls—one that in essence of course relates to the sale of narcotic drugs in both. A similar mood is prevalent in barbershops, naturally with a different, more confidential relationship. All professions devoted to direct care of the body, such as barbers, waiters, bathing attendants, and masseurs, share something like a similarity of caste. Above all, we will notice a lithe dependency here: while the barber is working on a beard, his political opinion is that of the person he is shaving at that moment. Nevertheless, he can also be influential—his means, in correspondence to the bodily proximity, is the insinuation, which is more difficult to resist than we commonly imagine. Indeed, at least once we have all made a run of unnecessary purchases on such occasions, and there also exist situations in which more important matters are involved. The political form in which this type is best able to express itself is despotism; it is also a form of transaction that regenerates in times of decadence. Places and regions in which we observe many flourishing temples of cosmetics are always remarkable, sometimes even fairytale-like. In the best establishments of this type, we easily slip into a mood of faraway or archaic things, for instance into an Asiatic or Satrap-like sense of comfort, such as only visits to Russian steam baths or the music of gypsy bands otherwise induce. We also enter more of a salon than a shop here; the service is silent, accommodating, and polite. Nothing is more rare than an uncouth barber. These circumstances naturally also possess their corresponding horoscopes; it is first and foremost the moon that exerts its influence here. Almost without exception, we meet with lunar countenances, pale, lymphatic, emotional; there is also a delicate inclination to adornment, to cultivation, to the highbred world. As in all lunar spaces, mirrors, crystals, and perfumes are in abundance. A sense of elegance, in particular for dainty footwear, and a vapid proficiency in learning languages is also often discernible. Smerdyakov in *The Brothers Karamazov* is a patent representative of this caste. Once I had been sensitized to this relationship, the affiliations became apparent to me on the street too. My best hit came on a trip from Naples to Capri, when I managed to classify a luxuriously dressed passenger with strongly affected good manners into this group. At dinner I sat next to him; he introduced himself as the director of a European hotel group and involved me in a discussion on suicide victims, whom he apparently viewed as the scum of humanity. "A single scoundrel like this can, and will, ruin a whole season!"

Incidentally, the practice of seeing in this manner is not limited to the pure enjoyment that it also undoubtedly provides. By and large, we categorize people into two broad classes, for example into Christians and non-Christians, into the exploiters and the exploited, and so forth. No one is free of this, because the bipartite is the most obvious of all divisions. Yet it should be taken into account that the bipartite is not a harmonious division—it is of a logical or moral nature. This nature entails that it always leaves a remainder; accordingly, in two-party systems, elections must happen again and again, or on the borders between Christians and pagans permanent war will reign. By contrast, stability grows to the extent that, beyond the spiritual separation, we are also capable of a substantial one, and the more numerous the compartments are, the more securely preserved will be that which we put into them. Herein lies the advantage of the caste system, which is defined by a bipartite as well as a multipartite division. The divisions of the horoscope also belong here.

A difficult but worthwhile investigation would examine whether our working world contains such germs, that is to say, whether a tendency to concentration of specific work characters can be observed. At any rate, it is not their simplification that contradicts the possibility of a multipartite division.

Red and Green — ***Goslar***

Shortly before sunset, a startling game of colors transfigured the city. All things red and yellow began to stir and awaken; they took on the hues characteristic of nasturtium flowers. The old tiled roofs in particular resembled bolsters of red chalk—overflowing reservoirs radiating their surplus light energy. Likewise, the landscape became more artificial, with all architectural and park-like elements emerging more forcefully. The spectacle was created by the city still receiving the light of the sunken sun from the high, red evening clouds, like from streetlights.

In a very similar manner, I have often observed that the color green is the first to revive at dawn. At this hour, it begins to flow into things with a silvery grace, like life force into the bodies of the convalescent. One sometimes gets the impression of a still-wet watercolor, in which a lane or a group of trees has first been handled with color.

This process appears to obey an underlying law, which also repeats in the course of the seasons. There the colors unroll in a sequence from the light greens of spring through to shiny, dense metallic glosses. These gardens are of sheer gold when autumn arrives. The same holds true for fruits, in which the ripening materializes in the transition from green to yellow or red. In this sense, violet, blue, and black are also only intensified reds.

Incidentally, this lighting seemed so extraordinary to me that in observing the faces of people on the streets, I was surprised to see that they were not alarmed by it. A particular fright lies in the awareness that one is alone in being affected by a significant spectacle. Of course, the converse has an equally powerful effect; for instance when we see the inhabitants of a city standing before their doors and talking about outlandish things. In such moments, I sometimes have the feeling that there must be a comet somewhere over the roofs.

Beach Passages (1) — ***Naples***

On my path to Cape Miseno and from there to Procida, the smell of the sea seemed deeper, more penetrating and invigorating than usual. Whenever I breathe it in as I follow the narrow fringe that is smoothed out by each retreating wave, I sense the lightness that betrays an increase in freedom. This could lie in the fact that this smell combines decay and fertility into one; creation and demise are maintained in equilibrium here.

This secret equality, which strengthens and comforts the heart, comes to expression above all in the enigmatic vapor from the seaweeds—the light-green gossamer, the black clusters, and glassy brown grapes—that the sea casts over the beach as a bed, onto which it scatters the colorful offerings of its abundance. There is much that finds its end here, and the wayfarer sees his path lined with decay. He observes white bodies of fish puffed up by putrefaction, sea stars drying up from the tips of their bright points into a discolored leather, mussels yawning their curved lips to receive death, and jellyfish, those glitzy floating eyes of the oceans with their gold-glimmering irises, fading so completely away that barely a skin of dried foam remains of them.

Nonetheless, there are none of the terrors here that warriors have left behind on battlefields, since these colorful quarry are incessantly licked by the sharp, salty, predatory tongues of the sea, which follow their spoor of blood and slurp them back in. Death here is connected to the springs of life, and so its odor resembles a bitter elixir that drives off feverish fears. Here too, to be sure, when the sea drones in the distance like in the large shell, which we took from the mantelpiece as children to put to our ears, and on whose rosy surface a flourishing disease seemed to form blue stains of mold—here too the proximity of death infuses those drops of poppy into our blood that leave us mournful and dreamy and bring to mind a dark carnival procession of destruction. Yet in return, the ray of life also touches our heart three times with its light, as from that mysterious black stone[15] that fires off red bolts of lightning.

This is the tangled scent of the flesh, invested with both the great symbols of death and creation and thereby most worthy of seasoning the border zone between mainland and sea.

At the Peepshow — *Berlin*

Amongst our memories, there are some of a peculiarly pictorial sharpness—we view episodes from the past as if peeping through keyholes or

15. Perhaps a reference to the black stone in the Kaaba at Mecca, which is said to have heavenly origins and symbolizes an intersection of the sacred and profane realms.

the round openings of the panorama show booths that were once set up at the annual fairs. When we are able to visually capture the little images that suddenly pop up as though a screen had been dropped, it becomes apparent that they do not concern events during which our consciousness worked under any special tension. Far more present to us are often those circumstances in which we participated in a vague, dreamy manner. For instance, an old woman takes us by the hand and leads us into the room in which our grandfather has just died. Memories like these often lie dormant for long periods; they are like film exposed with non-visible radiation, which we will one day be capable of developing. These include the erotic encounters, above all those that take place in an anarchic space.

I existed in a continuous state of fever; I had left the military hospital because lying had become intolerable, yet I was far from recovered.[16] In the morning, I sometimes still coughed blood into my handkerchief, but I tried to ignore it. I smoked strong cigarettes, the first of which I took from the bedside table on awakening, and wine also went quickly to my head.

During the night, I would occasionally be startled from sleep by gunfire; there were prisons in the convoluted little quarter where I had rented a room, and attempts were made to liberate prisoners. In some nearby barracks, a court martial was active, each day shooting the looters who had been caught the night before behind a monument. My landlady's children knew the schedule and eagerly attended the proceedings. Only a few steps from this monument, an amusement park had been erected; the carousel organs played from evening until dawn.

In the mornings, the streets looked bleak and run-down, the paving was all broken up; it was years since they had last been maintained. In the evenings, the picture changed; pulsating lights like those emitted by the physicists' vacuum tubes glimmered into life. The spectacle created the impression of a city in which the electricity grid had fallen into calamitous disorder, so that here and there the electricity flared up in colorful, wasteful short circuits. The blue, red, and green stripes blotted out the wretched, flaking façades and simulated the radiant portals

16. Jünger was gravely wounded in August 1918, shot through the lung, and he suffered the effects throughout the 1920s.

marvelous palaces. Behind them, there opened up dance halls, restaurants, and small cafés, in which a newfangled variety of enervating music was played. Whereas during the day a shabbily dressed, gray mass flooded through the streets, at night a clientele of overdone elegance gathered here, and whereas during the morning women could be seen waiting in long lines outside the bakeries, at night the buffets were laden with plates brimming with lobster and truffled fowl.

Life began only late, and during the afternoons the cafés remained almost empty. I used to meet with a tall, chestnut-brunette in one of them; we had become acquainted during the return of one of the home-coming regiments. A great contrast subsisted between the woolly fever in which I found myself and the sober resoluteness of this girl, whose unusual first name I have since forgotten. Her regular, somewhat prudish features suggested one of those gym teachers whose secret desire is a summer vacation to Sweden and who can be observed waiting for good novels in the library.

I don't remember our conversations; they must have taken place in two very distinct dialects. Like many of the home-comers, I was like a galvanic current that transforms the metals it touches, regardless of what images they have been imprinted with. A condition like this was of course particularly well suited to re-opening the age-old dispute that regards such couples: whether the drink is to be more cherished or the cup from which it is served. I felt myself impelled feverishly on by the maelstrom of the downfall; everything enduring, everything preserved and cared for, was onerous to me.

But it may have been precisely there that my charm lay, whose effect I sensed and exploited, as self-willed and intractable as a child that intends to follow its whim, come what may. In addition, there was the stupid amusement I felt in testing out this influence—like that which small-time hypnotists feel in giving their victims absurd tasks, whose accomplishment benefits neither them nor anyone else.

So too on this afternoon I had exhausted all possible torments to get her to come to my apartment—with a methodical persuasion that cost me far less effort than resisting it did her. But as soon as I tried to wrest away her coat, she shrank back with signs of fright in her face, like a sleepwalker coming to her senses; in the next moment, the door slammed behind her. Her movements happened as though under strong compulsion; they astonished me, as though I were watching her from afar playing a role whose meaning I did not really understand.

But I was still more astonished when I saw her come back into the room after a quarter of an hour, silent and without looking at me. She locked the door behind her and began to undress, without a word, and with a certain anger that expressed itself in the kind of sob we emit when a button or a zipper seems to resist our efforts. Without at all thinking about her coverings, she came toward me, and we stared at each other a long while—with tense and unquestionably hostile attention. I noticed that she fixated me with her glance; then her pupils began to dilate and she looked right through me like an uninvolved extra.

There exist words of such inconsequential profundity, or of such profound inconsequentiality, that one is almost ashamed to repeat them liberated from the living moment to which they are bound. It seemed to me as if there were yet a third party in the room, very carefully scrutinizing the scene, who abruptly commented in a matter-of-fact tone:

"You've been drinking wine."

And I heard myself answer in a quiet, scornful voice:

"And so? No harm done."

I could see us distinctly in an old, slightly skew mirror, as two figures lit by the dim glow of the coals; like the greenish gauze veil in front of a puppet show, the mirror's tarnished metal coating lent our contours an illusion of distance. And from a great distance, from the distance of a dream, came back:

"Oh yes, there is. There is harm done - - - a great deal."

The Chief Forester — *Goslar*

The vast forest that I was walking through was at once familiar and unknown to me. It consisted of regularly spaced woodlands that swarmed with city slickers on Sundays, but between them were scattered islands of primeval forest and uncharted mountain ranges. I had penetrated into its heart to call on the Chief Forester, since I had learned that he wanted to eliminate an adept who had gone hunting for the blue viper.

I met him in his gothic hunting salon, which came across like an armory. Traps hung from all the walls, which were entirely covered with nets, gins, mantraps, fish traps, and mole snares. A collection of artfully braided nooses and knots hung down from the ceiling—a tangled alphabet, with every letter captivatingly represented. Even the candelabra fit in with the decor: the candles were stuck onto the spikes of a large, ring-shaped spring trap. It was of the type that is hidden under dry leaves on a lonely forest trail in the fall, which at the lightest touch of a human foot snaps shut with a deadly bite at breast height. On this occasion however its fangs were hardly bared, since a wreath woven of matt-green mistletoe and red rowanberries encircled it in honor of my visit.

The Chief Forester sat behind a massive table of reddish alder that glimmered phosphorically in the twilight. He was occupied in polishing little swiveling mirrors of the kind used to entice larks in the fall. After he had greeted me, we immediately fell into a lively discussion on the hunting privileges on the hillsides of the blue viper. Since I noticed that he occasionally inconspicuously altered the arrangement of the lark mirrors in the course of the conversation, I remained very much on guard. His conduct in general was very strange; during long segments of our argument, rather than answering, he limited himself to pulling various decoy whistles from his pocket and producing whistles, cheeps, or tweets from them. But at significant turns in the conversation he always resorted to a large wooden cuckoo flute and puffed out chimes from it like a cuckoo clock. I understood that it was his way of laughing.

As involved as our conversation was, it kept coming back to the single same point. He emphasized over and over:

"The blue viper is the most important thing in my forests—it lures all the best game into the hunting grounds for me."

And over and over I tried in vain to appease him:

"But the slopes on which the blue viper lives are never frequented by people."

It seemed that this objection particularly amused him, because as soon I brought it up, he repeated his mad cuckoo call almost interminably. Since Nigromontanus had sharpened my ear to the obsolete figures of irony, I wisely refrained from a reaction.

Long did we argue back and forth in enigmatic sentences, which occasionally crossed over into pure sign language. Finally the Chief Forester broke the discussion off:

"I see that in hieroglyphic dominoes you are indeed a match for me. Since old Gunpowder Head,[17] you're the first that can give it a go here. But climb up to the slopes for yourself once, then you'll realize what is going on up there!"

So I went on my way, guided by the ruckus from deep in the pines of the fire hen,[18] one of the Mauritanians' heraldic animals. With the sun at its apex, I left the forest and entered the hot, barren cirque, whose ground was entirely overgrown with low thistles. They were of the stemless variety, jagged like an earthstar,[19] which we call carline thistles.[20] Wood spurge was also sparsely mixed in. Scores of narrow, age-old paths ran crisscross in all directions through the underbrush. Blue vipers blocked every one of them. When I saw the creatures, I became very merry and thought: "There! It's immediately obvious that the old fox is also playing with far too economical means." I concluded this from the fact that their bodies had been twisted into a lock knot, whose meaning could only be overlooked by a novice in such scheming. Nevertheless I hid myself behind a bush and lay in wait through the afternoon, naturally without seeing anyone.

Near evening, a women as old as the hills appeared with a small scoop in her hands. She hunched down over the open area and with her utensil scratched a rectangle about the size of a tabletop in the ground. Then she stepped into it, dug out a clump of earth from each corner, said a spell to it, and tossed it away over her shoulder. With each throw, I saw the steel flash like a little mirror.

This procedure filled me with such curiosity that I forgot all about the locking knot, crept up quietly behind her, and whispered to her:

"Hey, little mother, what are you up to there?"

She turned around without a trace of surprise, as if she had been expecting me, looked at me, and whispered back with a titter that made my blood run cold:

17. Most likely a reference to Friedrich Nietzsche.

18. *Feuerhenne*: a folk name for the black woodpecker, as related by Jünger in *Strahlungen I* (April 28, 1940). Its coloration is black with a red head, thus suggesting, in addition to the Mauritanians mentioned, perhaps also the NSDAP.

19. *Wetterstern*: *Astraeus hygrometricus*, or false earthstar, a mushroom whose fruiting tissue splits open in a star-like manner that is suggestive of a swastika.

20. *Eberwurz*: *Carlina acaulis*, a stemless alpine thistle with a large, spiny flower head. It can be eaten like artichokes and is thus called *Jägerbrot* ("hunter's bread") in German. Its appearance bears a resemblance to certain Nazi insignia.

"Oh don't you worry about that, sonny—you'll find out soon enough!"

With terrifying clarity, it dawned on me that despite everything I had yet fallen into the Chief Forester's trap. I began to curse my cleverness and the secret overconfidence that had gotten me involved in such company, because I saw too late that all the subtleties of my operations had only served to make the threads with which he encircled me invisible. I myself was the adept he wanted to destroy, I was the game that had been lured in by the blue viper!

The Inventor ***Überlingen***

Onboard, day one in the dining room. As always at this time, the voyage passes by the Maldives, and as always, as soon as the swordfish appears, a cross fire of toasts and jibes flares up. Naturally, no secrets are revealed, because the preparation of the fish alla Cremonese means a new admission must have happened while on land. Indeed, a tiger lily bouquet blazes on the captain's table, and behind it the newcomer peeks through, a small, unpleasant fellow with pig's eyes. Evidently the ballotage must have been barely visited for a character like this to have slipped through without being given a white ball by someone.[21] As I reflect on this, he sends me a note through the steward, whom he indelicately makes march in goose step. He requests the honor of a preliminary introduction; his name must certainly be familiar to me already, for he has introduced a record-setting propeller onto all ships in the world. And so, like it or not, I have to rise and call for a toast in his honor, to which the rest of the company dourly join in. Now the little chap is seized by bravado, he stands up and begins to boast, relating among other things an inflation that he once instigated in Paris. As proof thereof, he points to his tailcoat, adorned with the red rosette of the Legion of Honor and which he had tailored for a trifle: "and this is a tailcoat that any tailor would charge three times the price for"—with this he turns around and presents us with an enormous protuberance. Our laughter fires him up into

21. "Ballotage," an anonymous voting method of the Freemasons using black and white balls to elect new members. In contrast to this text, the black balls indicated "no" in the Freemason's process; but since it is unlikely that Jünger would make such an obvious mistake, he probably intended a perversion or inversion of meaning or value, similar to the reversal of the swastika's direction by the NSDAP. Later references in the text to goose-stepping and to a black and red ribbon worn by the "Mauritanian" doctor strengthen this allusion to the NSDAP.

dancing with little bowing and shuffling steps between our tables; but then in the middle of a spin, he keels over. He has swallowed a fish bone, something that can easily happen to someone when the preparation of the Cremonese is unfamiliar. Right away our little doctor appears, with the black-red-black ribbon of the Mauritanians under his hastily thrown-over operating gown. He grasps the situation at a glance, because the incision he makes looks more like a battle wound, extending deeply down the entire length of the coat's breast. The company watches half-delighted, and half-peeved because their appetite has disappeared.

The Complaints Book ***Leipzig***

Dreamed that I was waiting for a connection in a small, remote train station that flies were buzzing around in. Since the miserable condition of the waiting room annoyed me, I sought to vent my bad humor on the clerks; I confronted them, pretentiously demanding this and that. Eventually they brought over the station director, who meekly apologized and begged me to refrain from making an entry in the complaints book. Since I had no intention of allowing his evasions, he was finally forced to bring it out and I prepared myself for a nasty epistle. However all sorts of obstacles then materialized: the ink was dried out, I had to ask for a penholder, and other similar things. The affair gradually transformed, so that the clerks got the upper hand; now they threatened me with measures, I had to present my ticket and identification, I missed my train and got mixed up in a thousand other hassles.

This could be further elaborated, for instance that the clerk began forcing the complaints book on me and insisting that I make entries, from whose letter strokes the aggravations then multiplied like a swarm of ants.

In the Greenhouses ***Dahlem***

In the afternoon, I made my usual circuit of the greenhouses in order to expand on my "Review of the Orchids," for which I have set a rule of play that the flowers be critiqued as actresses. The exercise consists in observing them with a lengthy, thoughtless gaze, until the appropriate expression for them arrives, as it were through spontaneous generation.

In this manner, I have discovered that the *Cattleya* can be compared to a Creole, while the *Vanda* manifests the superior counterpart, the

Malayan. The *Dendrobiums* are magic lanterns of cheerfulness, and the *Cymbidiums* are masters of the ciphers that reiterate in the grains of woods. I saw the most beautiful examples of all in the Parque Indígena in Santos, though not very close up. Above all, the *Stanhopea* invites us to linger awhile—as with the tiger lily, beauty and danger interpenetrate here, though the grandeur is lacking.

While I was occupying myself with these meditations, a troop of blind children holding hands in groups of twos and threes was guided through the greenhouses. I tagged along and noticed that they were given potted plants, whose flora they smelled and touched. The plants for which they made especially long pauses were mainly unremarkable plants for the sighted; for instance, they drew each other's attention to a New Zealand *Pseudopanax* that had hard leaves with spear-like serrations. In general, it struck me that they lingered longest in the Australian section, probably because the sculptural quality of the plants increased with the dryness.

It at once became clear to me that the blind must have a particular relationship to dryness. Accordingly, they do not perceive the sun as light but as warmth, and they are closer to sculpture than to painting; so too Breughel's famous painting, in which the blind tumble into the water as into a hostile element, has its own special profundity, and it is probably also significant beyond the external causes that Egypt is a land of eye diseases.

But most surprising of all was the behavior of these children in the cactus section; here they broke out into loud laughter, as their sighted companions do in front of the monkey cages. Their laughter was extraordinarily uplifting to me—it was like seeing grass and flowers growing even up on difficult terrain, such as high up on castle ramparts.

Frutti di Mare **Naples**

Over the past few weeks I have settled in here, as Dottore Pescatore, what the locals like calling the zoologists who work in the aquarium. Situated in the middle of a park stretching along the seashore, it is a cool, monastic place in which fresh and salt water gurgles day and night in great glass tanks. From over my worktable, my glance rests on Castell dell'Ovo, a stronghold the Staufer erected out on the water, and further back, in the middle of the gulf with its form reminiscent of an elongated snail, lies the beautiful Capri, where Tiberius once presided with his wantons.

Many of my favorites have lived in Naples, among them such diverse characters as Roger of the Normans, Abbé Galiani, King Murat, who wore his medals in order to attract enemy fire, and with him, Fröhlich,[22] whose *Forty Years in the Life of a Dead Man* is one of our most entertaining life histories. The splendid Burgundian de Brosse and Chevalier de Seingalt[23] also had things to say about the fine hours they passed here.

My own attention is dedicated to a small squid named *Loligo media* that each morning enchants me anew with the beauty of its colorful swan song, which it composes from a fluid spectrum of brown, yellow, violet, and purple tones. I especially love its delightful manner of fading out, a bit of nervous distraction that it uses to prepare new and undreamt-of surprises. All too soon, this splendor falls prey to death; it goes out like flaming clouds dissolving into moisture, and only the deep green-gold rings that gild its large eyes shine on like rainbows. Life plays its inebriating melody on this hand-sized body; it showers its surpluses on it, and then leaves it in the lurch like a heartless lover. After such magnificence, what remains is like a bloodless specter, the burned-out casing of a golden firework.

Incidentally, like its brother the great squid, its cousin the long-armed octopus, and the sepia with its pearly iridescence, this creature enjoys high culinary repute in these parts; and so as to experiment on it with every possible means of knowledge, I had it grilled in the manner of its connoisseurs and served with white Capri wine. It reappeared transformed into a plate of tender, oil-browned rings, next to which the ten-armed head lay like a closed water lily flower, or a fragment of a little mythological figure. My first suspicions were confirmed: the secret harmony that pervades all aspects of a being was also revealed in the taste; even with closed eyes, I could have very confidently classified the origin of this morsel into the zoological system. It was not crab or fish that betrayed itself here, but rather mussels or snails, yet with the distinctly

22. Pseudonym of Johann Konrad Friederich (1789–1858). His autobiography first appeared anonymously in 1848–49 under the misleading title *Vierzig Jahre aus dem Leben eines Toten*.

23. Giovanni Jacopo Casanova (1725–1798), the Italian adventurer whose memoirs detail his sexual exploits.

expressed idiosyncrasy that behooves an ancient family. This flavor cannot be left out of the Bouillabaisse, the thick Marseillais soup that gathers the choicest fruits of the Mediterranean into a saffron-seasoned bouquet.

Each afternoon here, an assistant collects lists on which we indicate the "materials" we would like to observe. Many delights are hidden behind this prosaic word, because luscious desires can be indulged in behind the mask of the Latin species and genus names; and I don't know how amused the amiable Professor Dohrn would be if he discovered what sort of parasite had infiltrated the cells of his scientific beehive. The pure observation of formed life affords a pleasure that makes the hours fly by like minutes. The mind also strays into regions in which the surplus[24] is frightening; it then resembles a traveler who has lost himself in an archipelago from which no compass can lead him back out.

This list-writing provides a thrill like that of the Christmas wish lists children entrust their dreams to. The station's steamboat gets underway before daybreak, and by the morning hours the catch is brought back to the workplace in glass jars and shallow bowls. A fine gauze net is used to fish out the water's floating life forms, the raw material of the waters of the gulf, which is itself like a great, rich soup bowl—a world of glassy filaments, rods, and tiny spheres. Dragnets with heavy wires have cropped the carpet of algae and been fattened with the myriad forms that live and prey on each other in these colorful meadows. Something extraordinary also always turns up in the mix, something seen for the first time like the pointy colored decoration atop a Christmas tree—a scarlet-red ring annelid writhing like a dragon on Chinese porcelain, a fragile saffron-yellow feather star of delicate radial symmetry, a little transparent crab that lives in a small gelatin drum, a Venus girdle with a green-violet spark oscillating in its crystalline body, or a shark egg in which the breathing young can be seen, slumbering as if in a pillow of glassy keratin from which the fastening tendrils dangle down.

The secrets concealed in these southern seas exert an inexhaustible attraction for a northern eye accustomed to paler lusters. The colors of terrestrial creatures, insects for instance, also gain in richness and variety in warmer regions; they become more flamboyant and metallic,

24. *Überfluss* in the original. See also "The Surplus" in this volume.

more provocative and sharply set off against one another. Yet only the sea confers to its inhabitants that playful elegance and softness of tone, that iridescent, lively flux of old glass, that wonderful tenderness and intimacy of the ephemeral. Its tones are dreamier and belong more to the night than the day; they need the deep blue abyss for protection. In the deep violet and dark red patches that are baked into tissues resembling fine white, pink, or yellowish types of porcelain, the colors sometimes recall certain varieties of orchids, like the *Stanhopea*—these also seek out the steamy, uniform, dark-green nights of the deepest forests. There is really something marvelous in the fact that this brilliance animates just the most delicate and moist of life's creations; in the same manner, it also issues from the most precious and vulnerable organ of the human body, the eye.

A work space like this, in which life is gathered in so many forms, begs comparison with a clockmaker's workshop, in which small and large clock hands revolve over hundreds of painted dials. Regardless of which clockwork its glance falls on, the eye beholds an exceedingly ingenious achievement, be it the umbrella of a medusa opening and closing with the rhythm of breath, or the tiny vesicle in the body of a single-celled organism pulsing with a heartbeat. All of these pendulums, of longer or shorter periodicity, swing from the point that is at the center of all time. Being surrounded in this manner by the ticking of life clocks consequently imparts a sense of security; and here I share the taste of the Prince of Ligne, that endearing knight and warrior in the blood, whose castles, on whose roofs white doves rested, were built in the middle of broad pleasure gardens, with nest-filled shrubs, densely inhabited pastures, flower beds swarming with bees and butterflies, and ponds whose mirrored surfaces trembled continuously with the ripples of plump, rising carp.

This truly means to be surrounded, like by sentries, with allegories of life.

The Beach Walk — *Berlin*

Walking on the beach with the islanders along a deserted stretch of coast. In the body of an enormous fish thrown up from the sea, we discover a dead person, whom we extract like a newborn from the brownish mass of flesh. A man in a blue seaman's jacket requests my silence and highest circumspection: "An evil find. Don't you know that one of his last, most terrible moves is to disguise himself as a corpse and get washed up on shore?" A sudden sense of fear, as the beach gets more chaotic and bleak. A hurried retreat through an oak forest, past a thatched farmhouse in which the Old Hag lives. We do not get by unnoticed, for her tame sparrow hawks accompany us, fluttering alongside in the bush. A secret correspondence between the sparrow hawks and the dead person. When we snatch a last look back from the edge of the forest, we are shocked by a butchery that is taking place on the farmstead. Before an open barn door, farmhands have staked the body of a powerful man onto a board with his legs upward; the flesh is repulsively white, already scalded and shaven. The head swims in a steaming trough; its full black beard makes the sight even more frightening. The beard adds an animalistic element; it awakens a feeling something like this: there must have been a real, strenuous battle, in which the schnapps had not been spared.

A terrifying pursuit by the Old Hag follows, during which we dodge here and there, while she takes the shortest path to get at us. The mechanism of these intricate and thrilling movements signifies the battle of good, in which we seek refuge, against evil. But because we are not good from the ground up while the Old Hag is thoroughly evil, we can only succumb. This fatal necessity is expressed in the Old Hag's steady gaining of ground. A rising sense of fear eventually completely washes the images from the tissues.

The Song of the Machines — *Berlin*

During a stroll last night through the outlying streets of the eastern district where I live, I came across a dark and forsaken image. A barred cellar window opened up a view into a machine room, in which a monstrous flywheel spun on its shaft, quite without human supervision. While a warm, oily haze wafted out through the window, my ear became captivated by the marvelous working of a confident, controlled energy, which, as quietly as if on panther's paws, took possession of my senses. It was accompanied by a fine crackling, like that discharged from the black coat of a cat, and the drone of steel whistling through the air—this was at once a little soporific and at the same time highly stimulating. Here I again had the impression one gets sitting behind the engines of an airplane, when the throttle lever is thrust forward and the terrific roar surges up of powers that want to break away from the earth; or when plunging by night through a cyclopean landscape, where the darkness is torn open by the fiercely blazing flares of blast furnaces, in the midst of a frenzied activity where it seems inconceivable that even a single atom is not at work. High above the clouds and deep in the belly of the glistening ship, a proud and painful feeling takes hold of us as the power pours through the silver wings and the iron ribs—a sense that the ultimate stakes are now in play,[25] whether we are steaming along in a luxury cabin as opulent as an oyster shell, or lining up an adversary in our crosshairs.

It is difficult to form a clear picture of all that is at stake here, because solitude is one of its preconditions and the collective character of our times obscures it even more. And yet everyone today takes their place, unceremoniously and alone, be it behind the fire in a boiler room or in the responsible zones of thought. Inasmuch as man does not consider evasion and the times find him prepared, the great process is sustained. But what befalls him when he steps up to this challenge is difficult to describe; it may only be a general feeling, such as in the Mysteries, say that the air becomes gradually more charged. If Nietzsche marveled that the worker did not emigrate, then he mistook the weaker solution for the stronger one. A hallmark of everything being at stake is that no evasion is possible; a man's will might lead him to this point, but matters then consummate themselves under a compelling pressure, as in birth or dying. Our reality is thus beyond the kind of language with which the Miles Gloriosus[26] attempts to master it. In an action like that on the Somme, the attack was in fact a respite, an act of conviviality.

The steel serpent of knowledge has lain on ring upon rings, scale upon scales, and under the hand of man, its work has been invigorated in overpowering fashion. Over land and sea, it now stretches out as a blazing lindworm, which over here a child could almost rein in, while over there its fiery breath incinerates great cities. And yet there

25. The original phrase, *Das Gefühl, im Ernstfall zu stehen*, could also be rendered, in a manner suggestive of the decisionism of Carl Schmitt, as "a sense of existing in a state of emergency."

26. Miles Gloriosus: stock dramatic character of the boastful soldier, derived from ancient Roman comic theater and later used by Shakespeare (Captain Parolles in *All's Well That Ends Well*) and in the Commedia dell'Arte (Il Capitano.)

are moments in which the song of the machine, the fine humming of electrical current, the trembling of turbines in the cataracts, and the rhythmic explosions of motors seize us with a more secret pride than that of a victor.

Vicious Books — *Berlin*

The Marquis de Sade's *Philosophie du Boudoir*,[27] which was circulated in illegal prints for over a century, contains things elsewhere unheard of as material for the pen, if we are to exclude graffiti on the walls of dirty dark corners. It is the product of a mind that read above and beyond its Rousseau and drew the consequences, a prose that stands in relation to the powdered and Diavoletti-speckled forms of Crébillon,[28] Couvray,[29] or Laclos[30] like a broad battle axe of the Septembriseurs[31] to the knights' epées. It echoes the howl of the werewolf that hunts voraciously through the sewers, with damp, clammy fur and an insatiable hunger for flesh, in the end swilling blood and devouring the offal of life. Each swig from the red cup is seawater that only makes the thirst more maddening.

To this corresponds the manner in which the pen is wielded: for example, the use of dashes to separate the words and snatches of sentences, so that the diction is robbed of its breath and torn up into rattles and groans; so too the endless stringing together of synonymous words for actions and objects, which are thereby to be groped at ever more plainly and hungrily—the language bores its red-hot spines into the flesh; also the quotation marks used to brand any arbitrary phrases as dirty jokes—an absolute assumption of a vile accord with the reader; and finally, a way of using genteel expressions to interrupt the naked

27. *Philosophy in the Bedroom* (1795), an erotic book by the Marquis de Sade, written in the form of a dramatic dialogue.

28. Claude Prosper Jolyot de Crébillon (1707–1777) was a French novelist who wrote, among other works, *Le Sopha, conte moral* (1742), an erotic political satire that forced him into temporary exile from Paris.

29. Jean-Baptiste Louvet de Couvrai (1760–1797), a French novelist, playwright, journalist, politician, and diplomat.

30. Pierre Ambroise François Choderlos de Laclos (1741–1803), a French novelist, official, and army general, best known for writing *Les Liaisons dangereuses* (*Dangerous Liaisons*), a masterpiece of eighteenth-century novelistic literature exploring the amorous intrigues of the aristocracy.

31. The September Massacres, a wave of mob violence that overtook Paris during the French Revolution in 1792.

brutality of the deeds, thereby lending the passages of the wildest melees the ultimate degree of visibility through an unexpected flash of prudery.

The whole thing is an alarming read, due less to its horrors than to the perfect assurance with which it breaks the hidden covenant that exists between human beings. The impression made is as if someone in a room were to raise their voice to say, "Now that we animals are gathered here alone…"

An illuminating link has been preserved here in the form of the nearly lost novel *Le compère Mathieu, ou les bigarrures de l'esprit humain*[32] by Dulaurens, who ended up in prison as a publisher of atheistic books. Pater Johann makes an appearance in this book, a character in which Rousseau's virtue has already very clearly budded the bestiality that is one of its hidden basic qualities. Its antipode is Voltairian brilliance.

Utterly contemplative and far from all base emanations of the will is the cruelty in Octave Mirbeau's *Jardin des Supplices.*[33] It enhances the luminosity of the colored world like a dark fabric bearing silken blossoms. Strollers through its lovely gardens pass viewpoints where Chinese torture masters can be seen at work; at the sight of these agonies, a strangely potent sense of life is awakened in the heart. The colors and sounds call forth deep, voluptuous sensations, the flowers in particular pouring out unearthly fragrances. The spiritual action performed here by the author is to polarize: lust and agony, normally more or less uniformly distributed, stream here toward two opposing poles, and whereas at the one the image of man writhes in the dust, at the other it appears to stride forward, as though of a higher life.

It is likely that alongside the blind fury of the masses, a sentiment similar to this was alive in the refined levels of the Roman circus—the exaltation that a man feels when he believes himself to be acting on behalf of destiny. And yet the veiled images of the gods indicate that an awareness of the base, demonic nature of the indulgence was in fact present.

In our own cities too, we sometimes encounter types who give us the impression they might revel in the agonies of others, and we always

32. Henri Joseph Du Laurens (1719–1793), a French novelist, author of *Godfather Mathieu, or the Debaucheries of the Human Spirit* (1787), not translated into English.

33. Octave Mirbeau (1848–1917), a popular, avant-garde French journalist, art critic, travel writer, pamphleteer, novelist, and playwright, among whose many works is *The Garden of Tortures* (1899).

find that this involves spirits who are in one way or another enchained, be they the rabble wasting away as if in dungeons, or others of an Asiatic way of life onto whom there readily clings something of the vacuous effeminacy of steam baths. The moment order begins to falter, particularly in breaks between two historical periods, these forces break out of their cellars and corners and from the limits of their private debauchery. Their aim is despotism, more or less intelligent as the case may be, but always modeled on patterns from the animal world. In their speeches and texts, they therefore also like to confer animal traits on the victims they seek to destroy.

This consuming impulse is opposed by an attitude that can be best characterized as that of goodwill, and it graces the powerful and the simple alike. This goodwill is like a light by which alone the majesty in a person appears in its true form. It is closely connected with the noble and sovereign aspects in us, but also with our free and creative power. It reaches back into distant times; and it adorns Homeric heroes no less than the age-old kingship that once passed its judgments in the open market. Here it represents the spiritual aspect of power that is based on good origins, whose symbol is not the purple cloak but the ivory staff.

Wherever this free and luminous space exists between men, as good law vouchsafes it, there the images and forms also flow effortlessly forth. It creates a favorable climate for the flourishing of civilized behavior in particular; and thus constituted, small cities have attained to greater significance in the history of our planet than vast kingdoms in which countless millions eked out their existences. In the same way, a tiny garden easily produces a richer harvest than a vast wasteland.

It bodes well for us that our memory orients history by these stars of the first magnitude. In this respect, we are indeed like astronomers who are dependent on what is visible, because just as only a mighty light penetrates the endless distances, so only a superior consciousness comes through the fog banks of time. There exists a degree of illumination that overcomes the attenuating effect of the centuries—thus the Athens of Pericles is more visible to us than the thousand-years-more-recent Athens of the Middle Ages, for which Gregorovius gathered up the meager historical fragments.

When we consider the force with which the wastelands and monstrosities have pushed forward time and time again, it will always be astonishing that the models and paragons have been conserved through the millennia in all their luminosity. In this respect, the Odyssey is the great song of shining reason, the ballad of the human spirit, whose path leads to its goal through a world filled with elemental horrors and terrifying ogres, indeed even against the opposition of the gods.

Beach Passages (2) — *Zinnowitz*

In the dense brush behind the dunes, in the heart of a lush reed belt, I bagged a lucky image during my usual walk: a large leaf from a trembling aspen, in which a circular hole had been broken through. From the edge of this cut-out, a dark green fringe seemed to hang down, which upon closer observation turned out to be composed of a row of tiny caterpillars that had clasped themselves by their jaws onto the leaf pith. A butterfly's eggs must have recently hatched here, and the young brood had spread like wildfire over their feeding ground.

The unusual element in this sight lay in the painless nature of the destruction that it presented. The fringe gave the impression of consisting of dangling fibers of the leaf itself, which seemed not to have lost any of its substance. It was very evident here how the double accounting of life is reconciled; I had to recall the words of consolation that Condés gave to the weeping Mazarin over the six thousand fallen at the Battle of Freiburg: "Pah, a single night in Paris gives life to more people than this whole campaign has cost."

The attitude of this commander, who sees the change taking place behind the burning, has always struck me as a sign of a healthy life that does not shy away from a bloody incision. It is concentrated, with all the classical conciseness that so irritated Chateaubriand, in *consomption forte*, strong consumption, a phrase that Napoleon occasionally muttered during battles at those idle moments for him when all reserves were on the march, whilst the front withered under the attacks of cavalry squadrons and the fire of advancing artillery, as under a surf of steel and flame. These are words one hates to miss, sparks of soliloquies from furnaces that glow and tremble, as the spirit is distilled from steaming blood into the essence of a new century.

Underlying this language is a kind of faith in a life that knows no empty spaces. At the sight of its fullness, we are allowed to forget the hidden sign of pain separating the two halves of the equation—as the gnawing work of jaws here separates the caterpillars and the leaf.

Love and Return[34] ***Leisnig***

I landed as an officer with a crew of castaways on an island in the Atlantic Ocean.

We were all very ill and so were taken into the care of a nun in some wooden huts in a small fishing village that had been erected amidst the stone ruins of a razed city. Along with the woes that scurvy and exposure brought us came the peril of a narcotic plant that grew on the island and bloomed at twilight. Its yellow, phosphoric heart was surrounded by a ring of ruddily glowing false-flowers; at the sight of the plant, one felt the temptation to eat from it. But anyone who tasted it fell into a sleep from which he could never again be awakened.

In a long, low shed in which nets were hanging out to dry, we had laid out a row of these deathly sleepers. They were feverish and breathed heavily; changing dreams could be seen flitting across their faces. The nun endeavored to make their beds comfortable and to get a little soup into them, and I helped her out with this. Through the solidarity of this cheerless work, we grew very close; I was initiated by her into some of the secrets of the island and given small objects that had washed up on shore from wrecked ships.

In the course of time, I seemed to recognize more and more clearly that I was linked through age-old relations with the nun and with the island. In the short breaks that the work permitted, I gladly pondered this, thoughtfully but without passion, as if reflecting on the pages of a book that one reads when not on watch. One evening, after we had again been giving care all day, I walked up and down on the small seaside meadow in front of the huts to get some fresh air. The sense of connection glowed up still more vigorously within me, like a melody that the mind has forgotten but that still stirs within it. Then I saw the starry blossom of the plant begin to glow, and although I recognized the danger, I was overcome by the fatal curiosity of memory and so broke from it and ate.

34. *Wiederkunft*, translated here as "return," may be a reference to Nietzsche's idea of the "eternal return," for which he used both *ewige Wiederkunft* and *ewige Wiederkehr*.

In an instant, I was cast into a magnetic sleep. The same time that casts us out into life sucked me back in and I was transposed into another condition. I found myself once again on this island, on which a stone city now stood in place of the huts. I fancied that I recognized a form of early Gothic in its style, but one that had deviated in a fantastic manner by way of a lengthy, concluding evolution. The lancet arches had constricted into narrow crenels that were surrounded by sculptures of fabulous sea creatures. It also seemed to me that kelp had taken over the pattern-creating effect normally assigned to the rue. Thus the windows of the large mother church ran across the walls of white coral limestone like a network of dark green bands. Their light suffused the interior with a cool submarine radiance, in which the gold of countless votive paintings gleamed as if from sunken treasures. The walls were completely covered in name boards and figureheads from plundered ships. Between them were scattered paintings of burning or sinking vessels, on whose decks the last moments of a horrific carnage played out, never without the helping and redemptive presence of the Holy Virgin of the Sea, whose lovely apparition, draped with clouds or Saint Elmo's fire, was depicted high up over the masts.

The island was now inhabited by a colony of Christian buccaneers, who occasionally ventured into far-off seas in search of booty. I found myself a guest of these people, who were very amenable whilst on their island home, and I lived in the house of the first captain. A great unrest prevailed in the city, because increasingly specific reports confirmed that this previously unknown island had been uncovered as a pirates' nest and that a mighty Spanish flotilla was making sail for it.

I took no part in the defensive preparations being carried out all around, but sat rather in conversation with the captain's daughter in a room decorated with weapons. We spoke hastily and in great agitation, because we sensed that time was running out and that we still had very much to say to each other.

She repeatedly vowed to keep me out of the close combat. I on the other hand had decided to share the destiny of her people, and this all the more in that I felt that this danger was itself the best guarantee of keeping her. While we talked about this and that, her brother stumbled in: "The Spaniards are in the city!" In the same moment, a fiery glow came through the window, and its red gleam simultaneously saddened and exhilarated me, like a farewell drink. I grabbed a wheel lock gun that stood in the corner and ran out. Flames already lashed from the great tower that spiraled up like a seashell, and hordes of pirates with Spaniards on their tails were coming up from the harbor.

I laid myself down on a narrow strip of meadow, cocked my gun, and brought one of the pursuers down. His companions remained standing and shot at me; I saw the fire and the white smoke that blew out of the muzzles, then I felt the projectiles penetrate my body.

I remained on the ground and lost a great deal of blood. Then I noticed how the wonderful flower opened its crown beside me. I broke it off, ate of the petals, and fell asleep. With the very last shimmer of light, I realized: I would live countless times, meet the same girl, eat the same flower, and with that perish, just as this had already happened countless times before.

The Color Red — *Goslar*

We have reason to be cautious with the color red. In the flowing current of life, it emerges with economy, but it glows wherever there are tensions. It hints at that which is concealed and is to be concealed or tended, in particular fire, sex, and blood. Wherever red pops up, it thus evokes a sense of alarm, like the little red flags used to bar routes into stone quarries or shooting ranges. In general, it indicates the proximity of danger, and thus tail and hazard lights on cars are red. This is particularly true for fire hazards; fire alarms and hydrants are painted red, as are the vehicles in which flammable liquids or explosives are transported. With the rising demand for fuels and propellants, a grid of blazing red and yellow kiosks spreads over the world, the mere sight of which would allow a stranger to our world to understand that he finds himself in explosive territory, in an age in which Uranus begins to reign. Red is the preferred color for explosive materials; for the merely flammable ones, yellow and red-yellow signs are used.

The extraordinary duplicity that animates the world of symbols entails that this color is at once menacing and enticing. Its prestige is nicely expressed in the red berries with which hunters embroider their snares and nooses. With choleric animals like turkeys and bulls, the enchantment emerges in its most forceful form, as bedazzlement. A human temperament also exists that is driven to dizziness by burning reds, that of certain varieties of tulips for instance.

This urgent, inviting effect of the color red makes it seem particularly adapted for indicating things of the most immediate priority. This usually also coincides with what is dangerous, for example in the case of first aid kits, lifebuoys, or emergency brakes. Occasionally, it also concerns the element of abstract acceleration, for instance on the little red marks that the post office sticks onto express letters.

Its simultaneously menacing and soliciting character emerges most clearly where this color is involved in relations between the sexes. An oppressive spectrum exists here, from the sullen, smoldering light that illuminates the corridors of houses of ill repute and almost seems to touch one, to the garish, unabashed flesh tones of the carpets and draperies in the lobbies of large casinos and pleasure haunts.

In the red of lips, in nostrils and in fingernails, the color of our inner skin is revealed. So too we imagine the lining of clothes to be red, and we love it when this base color shines through in the slits and turnovers of the outer fabrics. This is the meaning of red cuffs, brims, collars, tucks, buttonholes, and of all red lingerie; the inner layers of beds are also red under the covers. This concept also extends into the interiors of rooms and houses with a special connection to pomp and ceremony. We enter ceremonial halls through red curtains, and red carpets are rolled all the way out to the driveway at receptions. We also like to line the boxes and cases where we keep jewelry with red silk. In this manner, the precious gift is showcased, while the splendor of the heavens and seas is simultaneously exalted: the pearl deserves the blue backdrop.

Among the remaining colors, yellow amplifies the unrest exuded by red; the red and yellow pattern elicits uncomfortable, flaming sensations. More malevolent still is red in combination with black, while green has the most tempering effect on it. A green background can even cheer it up, like the green turf does to the red cloth of a hunter's jacket, even though the connection to blood remains. An attenuating effect also happens with gray, whereas with white the blood aspect emerges powerfully through the contrast, for instance in the relationship between makeup and powder, wound and dressing, blood and snow. Showy power is accentuated by combining it with gold. As an additional element, white tends to the lovely, black to the proud and heavy-hearted. A sanguine vacancy is attached to pure crimson; like the sight of waterfalls or fireworks, it lays the chains of movement on our disposition. Remarkable are efforts to grow black roses from which the last trace of red has been distilled out through breeding. This is the philosopher's stone of gardeners, and in fact any form of knowledge must need be ill-disposed to red.

At any rate, we run a risk in wearing red, and so we usually like to display it as though it had become visible only through untidiness, through openings and breaks in our clothing, or as a displaced hemline. Those wearing broad, exposed swathes of red are possessors of deadly power, such as chief judges, princes, and generals, but also the executioner to whom the victim is delivered up. He is appropriately fitted with a black cloak, whose red lining becomes visible at the moment of the deadly blow.

The red flag of unrest suggests the inner aspect or the elementary substance of order. Hence it is not a real ensign, but rather materializes with the fire of the conflagrations and the spilled blood at those points where the woven covering has been torn. At times, the primordial red matter gushes forth as if from hidden springs or craters, and it appears to want to flood the world. But then it again ebbs, consumes itself, and remains over only in Caesar's toga.

Notes on the Color Red ***Überlingen***

I since came across a garden in Rio de Janeiro where courtesans draped in transparent silks were parading themselves on a terrace. Its barred gates were guarded by herculean blacks dressed in red livery, and a fiery carpet thrust itself down between a corridor of palms to the street. This triumph of lust as a mighty force of life came across all the more powerfully since its arena rose up in the middle of a slum. We Europeans only display our cannons this nakedly.

That the impact of the color red is best attenuated by green is due, among many things, to the compensation that occurs here between the moderate and the fervent colors of life. Green is the color of the plant world, in which life operates through gentler circulatory systems. Only in the sex organs, like in flowers and fruits and later in the seeds, does red push through more forcefully. Where reds and greens interpenetrate en masse, such as in flowering rose gardens, a sense of a lighter, loftier existence may arise. Thus we read reports of the marvelously exhilarating luminosity of Chinese parks that are honeycombed with paths of pulverized brick dust. In dark peonies, the distribution of red and green is unsurpassable. And then Egypt: a band of green in a red desert—human culture germinated in the Nile Valley.

But for red to become visible in its highest formulation, it requires blue as a backdrop. This becomes apparent when we behold a small red object on a blue surface.

Along the Canal — *Goslar*

Goslar is traversed by the Gose, a narrow watercourse that flows into the town at the Frankenberger Plan and leaves it again through the large water hole in the city walls. This weak point was once protected by the moat tower, an unknown but well-preserved building that is one of the treasures of the town.

Since old times, the part of the Gose lying within the walls has been called the "Abzucht"; as a designation for the exiting wastewater,[35] the name seemed ingenious to me. But as I later found out, it actually goes back via *Agetocht* to the Latin *aquaeductus*, which seems less fitting. This is a nice example of how the vernacular language digests a foreign word.

During my daily walk around the walls, I often turn in at the water tower canal and return along the Abzucht. Friedrich Georg,[36] who accompanied me today, called my attention to a form covered by the flowing water, which we at first thought was a stuffed toy made for children. However, at a closer observation, we discovered that it was a tiny lamb, whose umbilical cord could still be seen. A form that at a first quick glance had amused us instantly became repulsive, particularly as we recognized ever more clearly that it was in fact only the last emulation of a living form, an effigy composed of very fine sludge particles quivering in the current.

The discovery that a phenomenon, in this case of something charming, is only a projection and that fundamentally the void lies behind it is

35. *Zucht* in the original is literally "breeding," but *Abzucht* here could sound related to *abziehen*, to siphon or draw off (among many other meanings).

36. Friedrich Georg Jünger (1898–1977), a respected poet and essayist in his own right. Ernst Jünger considered him a brother in spirit as well as in blood.

not a new experience for me, and yet it always has something unsettling about it. Thus we sometimes look into eyes that consist of no more than cloudy, congealed mud, in which the most advanced stages of human lifelessness are revealed. The world today presents a new kind of horror, similar to that of stumbling across a drowned body—these are encounters in which a very specific theological situation looms up and for which a man needs the long-forgotten protection of severe purification measures. The reverse case, by contrast, in which the dead is revealed as living, has a cheering effect: we think we are looking at a piece of moldy wood, but a moment later a large grasshopper flies away, revealing a shiny second pair of wings beneath its gray wing covers.

The Tares of Fortune ***Leipzig***

I was sitting in the heart of a desolate landscape playing cards with a stranger. The table stood at the bottom of a sunken pit, a kind of sinkhole whose upper walls were striped with black veins of coal. I was about to stake a large bet, when the thought shot through my head: this character may not be playing an honest game. But then I said to myself: before sinking down to the bottom of the pit, this playing table must have been so long in use that countless games have been played out on its cloth. So if in fact this chump is not playing honestly, then this should have been exposed long ago. And since he must also have money, why should it run out, just when he is playing here with you?

These considerations, which went into far greater complexities—among other things, calling on the age of the rock strata in the pit for counsel and simultaneously reviewing the geology for its clues—flashed up like a light and just as quickly ceased. Uncertainty and improbability receded completely, so pronounced was the awareness of superiority.

Through such images it sometimes becomes clear to us that there is a particular kind of thought, perhaps a shorthand, that is able to grasp the element of similarity and resonance at its root and master it like a game. At that point, the sound of a single word suffices us to understand an unknown language. Drawn into the harmonious order, the very first object we catch sight of is transformed into a universal key.

This and nothing else also constitutes the allure of games of chance. A lucky run on the reds provides the player with more than money; it bestows on him a belief that we all have a deep need for—namely, to be in collusion, to have an understanding with the world. When the dice roll for us, or when a card is turned in our favor, we savor an exquisite pleasure—the enjoyment of a most secret, material intelligence. In fact, fortune is nothing but the elementary form of intelligence—in good fortune, the things, the world itself thinks for us.

This is the basis of the curious fact that we regard an opponent who triumphs over us through luck with a deeper resentment than another who rebuts us through intellectual superiority, for instance in a conversation or at the chessboard. We cheerfully raise our glass to toast our conqueror in a tournament, but the ring of fortune divides us more bitterly than Apollo's wreath. All men of the spirit are brothers, but the unlucky man is the stepbrother of the lucky one. He who sees what the world is able to offer its favorites feels his own misfortune all the more sharply. Something similar happens on the dance floor when the mere presence of an excellent dancer torments the awkward dancer and confirms his clumsiness—he is seized by the feeling that the whole world is laughing at him and that every object opposes him with its points and edges. A lucky person on the other hand is like a dancer whose steps are in perfect correspondence with the great world concert. He is like a character in the opera; his gestures, his words, and his expressions are arranged and led by a secret orchestra—his intelligence consists in letting a higher reason do the thinking for him.

A gambler is thus correct in attributing his losses to disruptions in the harmony of his arrangements. Even a change in the usual seating order or the appearance of a disagreeable person at the table can disrupt it. In such situations, any attempt to force a return of good luck through deliberation or systematic wagers leads to a quick ruin. He would do better to rely on a talisman, whose holder employs it like a magic compass that is to correct his direction. The loss of accord is first announced in the very perception of bad luck, and harmony cannot then be reestablished by any amount of effort—it would require knowing exactly where those specks of dust lie of which Napoleon said that a single one would suffice to throw him off course once his lucky star had gone out.

Those lives in which fortune returns and repeats are particularly instructive; time and time again, a man is attuned to the universe. These turns of fate are not uncommon in the lives of gamblers, but they can also be observed in those of princes and soldiers. In any case, the existence of these trajectories in a world where a single false step often suffices for ruin allows us to infer a strongly pronounced rhythmic intelligence. Such things are sensed in the fingertips, and indeed we will often observe that fine, well-formed hands point to fortunate circumstances. There is a science of the providential moment, and for those interested, Casanova's tomes provide insights here. These readings outweigh the old worn-out volumes of a hundred pedants; their great importance lies in allowing us to participate in an almost forgotten musicality of life. No efforts can match the alleviation that an era as such imparts when it carries any random little boat on its back. One fine morning a person wakes up as though in a house where everything from the cellar to the ceiling sings and swings. In such spaces, the forms generate and mint themselves, as if by magnetic force, with barely the touch of a finger.

At times, I get the feeling that the horn of plenty is beginning to tilt a little in our direction again, even if none of the living will enjoy its bounties. Our thinking still tills the earth too thoroughly for a clod of soil to remain behind for the delectable tares of fortune.

On* Crime and Punishment** ***Goslar

In *Crime and Punishment*, which I have just put down, one of the minor characters has become clearer to me, that of Luzhin, who is depicted as a variety of insect that takes part in the world of human relationships. The most repugnant aspect here is that this insect proceeds according to accepted patterns; it operates according to the rules of sound common sense and is equipped with an exact knowledge of what is just and equitable. Situations thereby arise in which it gains power over nobler but less prudent lives. Luzhin belongs to a type of cardsharp who knows how to take advantage when his partner plays inattentively. For example, Raskolnikov's sister and mother's anxiety over him puts this kind of advantage in Luzhin's lap. The repulsion he arouses comes from his embodiment of the capable type, who, as a mere technician of life, remains focused on his profit, which rarely eludes him, when in fact fundamentally different matters are concerned. He drops in on the afflicted as a usurer his debtors. In the game played with him, the double-dealing is accomplished not with false cards but by fraudulent stakes, because no winnings can issue from him and his kind. The significance of this figure lies above all in the fact that each of us, at some point in our lives, comes into contact with such a character, with the subordinate yet dangerous ascendancy that depends on understanding the mechanisms of life.

In the course of the storyline, the author then draws in the outlines of the character too strongly. Thus, in order to hurt Sonja, Luzhin allows himself to be swept into a blatant and clumsily arranged crime. But in precisely this manner he leaves the field of his strength, which rests on a better knowledge of the rules of the game. This also weakens the contrast between his and Raskolnikov's character. The dominion of the vulgar is most oppressive when it exploits the forms of the just and equitable. When it resorts to crime, the bitterness is mitigated.

In the novel as a whole, the convoluted architectural character is conspicuous—or better, the labyrinthine sensation that its reading arouses. With the exception of the Siberian section, this may be due to the almost complete absence of nature in the book. The storyline plays out in rooms, houses, streets, and bars, between which the involved parties rush to and fro in an unusually agitated manner. The actual course of the dealings seems to matter less than the spinning of a piece of life; everyone senses the urge to be connected to everyone else.

The frightening effect of its reading also has an architectural character—as though one were moving around at night in an unfamiliar house, without knowing if one will find the way out. Perhaps this explains why I quickly sensed the need to take measurements in the individual rooms. The method resembles that which we can use to protect us from the illusions of Indian sorcerers: by focusing our lens on the illusion itself, we remove ourselves from the direct effect of the spell.

It is also crucial for us not to lose the feeling of being a traveler. We take part in this drama as though we were wandering at night through the streets and squares of an unknown city, full of animation, among images of brilliant vividness. We peer into homes, into rooms and inns, but always through windows and doors, since everything greatly depends on us keeping the frames of these pictures in view. At times, we feel transported to applause, and then we begin to drowse off again, as if some narcotic essence were blown over us. The visions are unusually compelling particularly where the hideous is transfigured by a compassionate point of view. This begins right at the start, with the great confession of Marmeladov, the titular councilor; we seem to have been transported into a grimy kitchen, which smells of brandy and leftovers and whose floor is covered in the half-light with black cockroaches. But then we at once get the impression of being able to understand these animals' language; they fill the space with their sweet, grievous singing. But, be that as it may, we must never forget that we are in a foreign city, which we will leave the next morning and later only remember in our dreams.

Just how little we fundamentally have to do with these affairs, which we seem to spy on through a crack in the wall, the author knows even better than we. Thus it occurs to me that we generally tend to view the westerner, in the cast of the detective Porfiry, as the adversary in this world. Yet this antagonism is of a subordinate, psychological nature. The moment things get really serious, the dialogue continues in the native substance. The following is very indicative of this: when Raskolnikov decides to confess, it is not to Porfiry, who actually has sympathy for him, but rather to the highly unpleasant Lieutenant Gunpowder. Indeed, it is not a moral but a sacramental connection that is concerned here, which Porfiry would certainly like to extract himself from, as Pilate does in the Creed.

Raskolnikov occupies himself with a theory of power; the absurdity of his thinking lies above all in the relation to Napoleon, because all the while there are real figures moving in his vicinity that clearly have a connection to what we understand as power. Besides the priestly element, a royal one is suggested everywhere. This royal element emerges more distinctly in *The Brothers Karamazov* and above all in *Demons*, but it already sounds in *Crime and Punishment* in the exceedingly strange character of Svidrigaïlov. Whereas the basic material appears in fiery-fluid form in priestly natures like Alyosha, here it materializes at low temperature, and thus, like mercury at its freezing point, no longer allows a reading on the moral scale. A Russian counterpart to the Superman is suggested in these figures, a counterpart of perhaps greater reality.

This especially emerges in connection with goodness, which, for all its remoteness, has no theoretical paleness here. Instead, goodness, to stick with this term, undergoes a sort of museum-like reverence here; its powers are known, like those of an old, time-tested instrument that one takes up at one's pleasure to play lovely melodies on. One is equipped with an infallible instinct for the means of dealing out devastation among men. At the same time, the quantitative aspect, which would unquestionably diminish the depth of the enjoyment, is missing—it is not the capacity of the theater that determines the play. The contempt for mankind is more thorough, indicated above all in the manner in which things slide into disgrace; in this respect, Svidrigaïlov pulls off a powerful move even with his suicide.

Dostoyevsky presents these figures exclusively in a weakened state. Their prime must have occurred earlier, at a time when a feudal class surrounded by bondsmen attained individual freedom in single representatives, in otherwise intact conditions. It is therefore unlikely that this theme will be resumed in this sense at other points on the globe, though the attempts are not lacking. The race against skepticism is a hopeless one.

In the Utility Rooms ***Goslar***

I was sitting in a large cafe, in which a band was playing and many well-dressed guests were evidently bored. In order to find the toilets, I went through a doorway hung with red velvet, but then soon got lost in a maze of stairways and corridors and ended up leaving the elegantly decorated rooms for a badly run-down annex. I thought that I had come out at the bakery; the bleak corridor I walked through was dusted with flour and black cockroaches crept around on the walls. It seemed that someone was still working, since I came to a spot where a wheel was driving a belt with slow, jerky rotations; next to it, a leather bellows once in a while moved up and down. To see into the baking room, which probably lay below, I leaned far out of a blackened window that opened onto an overgrown garden. But the space that I then saw looked more like a blacksmith's shop. Each blast of the bellows sparked up a coal fire that had red-hot tools lying in it, and each revolution of the wheel drew in all sorts of machines. I saw that they had seized two guests, a man and a woman, and wanted to force them to take off their clothes. They resisted vigorously, and I thought to myself: "Well, as long as they still have their good things on, they'll be safe." But it seemed a sinister omen that the fabric began to give here and there from the grabbing and that the flesh was visible through the tears. I quietly withdrew and was able to find my way back to the café. I sat back down at my table, but the band, the waiter, and the pleasant rooms now appeared to me in a completely different light. I also understood that it was not boredom that the guests felt, but fear.

The Phosphor Fly ***Goslar***

Around midday in a plantation on the Steinberg, I observed a large, half-opened wasps' nest. In the process, a small fly caught my eye: it was black with yellow rings and in particular distinguished by two dazzling patches that shone like cat's eyes on the front of its thorax. These little creatures lurked around the opening of the nest, while the wasps buzzed in and out. They certainly harbored predatory intentions, whose execution I would have loved to spy on. Perhaps they even intended to sneak their young into the nest.

While thus engaged, I heard two young boys wandering by on the edge of the plantation. They were immersed in a metaphysical discussion, as children not infrequently are when there are no adults around. Unfortunately I only caught this one sentence:

"...you know what I think? What we live here is only dreamed; but after death we live out the same thing for real."

I quickly turned around to see the boy; it was the eleven-year-old son of a trail keeper who lived nearby. Children like this are naturally more sage than us. Sadly, such direct insight disappears as we watch; the voice change is the definitive moment. I can also clearly remember my own first metaphysical ideas; one of them was that I held adults to be actors, who did quite other things when amongst only themselves. Together with this, I held school to be a sham invented by them. Once, in seeing other older children with knapsacks walk by, I began to have doubts, but then I immediately thought to myself: "They've just been sent around, so that I'll continue believing—they'll throw their bags away around the next corner."

Incidentally, it occurs to me that when we eavesdrop on any arbitrary affair, for instance that of the wasps here, we simultaneously gain knowledge of other hidden things, like a hunter on his stand or a soldier at his outpost. My own first erotic episode was forced on me while playing hide and seek in an old house. When we begin to observe at any arbitrary point, we enter into a special relationship with the world as a whole, and when we comprehend one secret, many others also draw near, without our intention. This also holds true at a lower level for the inventor; one cannot decide to be an inventor, rather one becomes such by attaining the position of inventor. Consequently, people with this make-up often have a lucky hand in the most diverse fields.

Historia in Nuce: The Complement — *Goslar*

After we observe a certain color for a length of time, our retina generates its complement. Like every sensible phenomenon, this one also has its spiritual aspect, and from this we can conclude that our relationship to the world is given to us as a whole. If one or another aspect of the whole inordinately taxes our attention, the spirit summons up the missing part as a remedy.

At the same time, this relationship suggests a weakness in us, namely, that the whole is only comprehensible to us through the sequential nature of life. Initially we also perceive the missing element as the complementary color. We do not proceed in a straight line but in a wave pattern, and not from one step to the next but from one extreme to the other. We must regard these deviations as inevitable; they are part of life, which a pulsating element indwells, as is already apparent in breathing or the heartbeat. Yet our spiritual path resembles that of the hands on a clock, which are moved by the stroke and counterstroke of a pendulum.

So it is that we develop higher insights over the course of our life, or over successive generations, than in any of the particular moments from which these periods are assembled. If we keep this in mind, many contradictions in our nature can be understood. Thus, although we decidedly tend toward injustice, yet in the course of time we also come to see that which passion hides from us; our judgments become more apt. With all the daily inanities that we busy ourselves with, in our memory the important and the true always emerge more clearly. And however much we may be subject to the spirit of the times, we nevertheless at the same time put it to ceaseless trial on all counts. Thus there is inherent in us a tendency toward the complement, which has a healing effect.

This emerges with particular clarity in great historians: our history, which is one of parties, is complemented by a divine eye. Put in architectural terms, the historian draws into the Babylonian plan of our labors the arches that must necessarily escape the perception of the active powers, which are like the weight-carrying pillars.

The Zinnia ***Überlingen***

There are riches that come into our lives like gifts. One day we find them before us like images unfolding out of the invisible, and before long they are familiar to us, belong to us. This is what happened with the zinnia and me, a flower that migrated into our gardens a few years ago.

Besides the merits that gardeners normally find in it, the most surprising thing about this plant is the facility with which it uses color as a medium. Not only does it generate a rich scale of pure tones, as other garden flowers do, but it also has the unique talent of being able to develop a whole series of such color scales in different keys. Its blossoms thus appear to be tailored from and impregnated with vastly differing materials: ivory, fine skins, velvet, and cast bronze. This matches the plethora of pigments that are laid down on the petals, such as colored chalks and inks, but also oil, stone, and metal-based colors, and this moreover with numerous interpenetrations and mixtures.

A further augmentation is produced by the coloration of the undersides, which often become visible by a slight arching of each petal. In other cases, the color flows over onto the upper side, like ink over a wet edge. Be it through harmony or contrast, the components conjure up marvelous patterns. One very beautiful example: blossoms of deep velvet-red in the style of wallflowers, the individual petals with light-gold fringes overlapping each other like round roof tiles; and in the center, the residual non-metamorphosed stamens forming a golden button. This pattern is repeated in dark-brown, black, scarlet, and brick-red varieties, with the colors laid down now on a porcelain-like glossy foundation, now on a softly diluted one.

The deepest impression is created by these flowers where they emulate the colors of glowing metals, above all in the species that elongate themselves into flasks. Admittedly, they lack the shrillness, the rocket-like form that distinguishes some hyacinths, in particular the flame-flower, but in return the late moments of embers, in which warmth predominates over light, find expression in them. Scorching fumes then appear to shimmer around them, or the colorful sparks of freshly cast metal cores issue from them. This motif of slowly cooling ore is spun out in a multitude of variations by the concentric darkening of the light fringe colors. Such visions provoke a vibrant, almost painful joy, as the scalding contact reminds the heart of its relationship to the earth.

I notice that the zinnia is propagating itself into even the smallest gardens, though without the celebrity that once accompanied the tulips. It is a pity that Brockes did not know this flower; he would have created an everlasting flowerbed for it in his *Irdisches Vergnügen in Gott*.[37] When we behold a new flower, we understand the sentiment of the despot who offered a prize for the invention of new pleasures. We also gain a conception of the inexhaustible fertility of the world when we consider that all this glory originated from a pinch of seeds contained in a simple envelope. But soon its fresh colors are scattered over the earth, flung out like a shower of sparks.

Postscript to the Zinnia ***Überlingen***

While I usually only vaguely remember the circumstances in which I arrived at a new thought, my first impression of an image remains perfectly familiar to me—almost as though a different quality of time, a lighter and more transparent medium was involved, in which even the most distant things vividly retain their colors and outlines. I first saw the zinnia during one of my walks with Friedrich Georg at Muldenufer by Fischendorf, in a bloom that resembled a rosette of freshly minted and slowly cooling ducats.

Remarkably, memories like this also bring back the thoughts that occupied me at the time more distinctly; they stand there in the past like lights. In this case, the sight of the flowers interrupted a discussion on the impossibility of uninterrupted order in this world; and I credit my enduring memory of the details precisely to this interruption.

A greater security always emanates from images; they provide the foundation of memory. In all times and places it is vision that most powerfully animates the intellect; it is the prime source of all theory. Incongruities occur in the course of civilization when the spirit relies on sources of secondary or tertiary importance, for instance even in our sciences when that which has been recorded is indicated as a source. As a result, originality becomes a rare occurrence, and indeed in their usage, the words "rare" and "original" take on a similar coloration. By

37. Barthold Heinrich Brockes (1680–1747) was a German writer and poet of the early German Enlightenment. *Irdisches Vergnügen im Gott* (*Earthly Pleasure in God*) is an anthology of naturalistic lyrical poetry in which nature, in its beauty and utility, is reflected on as a mediator between God and man.

contrast, it should be remarked that a man is born original and that there exists a duty to keep him this way. Alongside the shaping and cultivating done by institutions, there exists a direct relationship to the world, from which primal power accrues to us. Our eyes must retain the power, if only for a moment, to see the works of this earth as if on their first day, that is, in their divine magnificence.

There are times—and perhaps also conditions—in which this gift is distributed to man like the dew that falls on the leaves. In others, the golden ether surrounding the images dwindles away and things remain behind in their merely conceptualized forms. A direct vision, in poetry for instance, can gain the immeasurable value of a wellspring in the desert here. Where language has petrified, a single verse may weigh as much as a library, and in these spaces the incomparable differences that Hildebrand arrogates to Dietrich von Bern are proven to be true:

--- The powers of the earth
Were given us in two halves
One to all the millions
The other just Dietrich alone.

From the Newspaper **Stralau**

"I have you at last, my beloved boys!"[38]

The morning newspaper recounted this final salutation of a mother before the coffins of her two sons. It gave me pause for long and diverse reflection. It seemed marvelous that in a period in which language finds itself in complete disintegration a simple woman was yet able to compose a sentence of such irresistible power.

The incident appeared among the miscellaneous news stories. Two young workers, brothers whose lives had already gone astray for some time, were surprised in the act of committing a crime, upon which a long chase followed. After a progressive tightening of the police net, they were eventually cornered in a house and brought down during a lengthy shootout.

I assume that the woman was first brought to her sons at the conclusion of the official procedures that follow on such cases. The police, the

38. In the original: "Hab ich euch endlich, meine lieben Jungen!"

district attorney's office, and the doctors had already completed their duties but were mostly still present, as were news reporters and certainly also the ever-present nosy onlookers.

In this awful position, in the face of both implacable public opinion and the official powers, it seems unthinkable that a father could uphold his affiliation. To stand his ground there, he would have to bring his own grief to the fore, or even more conspicuously distance himself by letting it be known, if not by his words then by his behavior, that his sons were unlike the rest of the family.

The mother's words, on the contrary, concern only the material and substantial affiliation; the sons are identified and acknowledged in them, and it remains irrelevant for the salutation whether in a moral-legal sense good and virtuous people or murderers and robbers are concerned. Not only the distinction between the tragic and the merely sad emerges here in the clearest possible form, but also that between the tragic and the moral world.

At the same time, a clear superiority over the official realms of order is revealed in the sentence—a form of gravity that cannot be restrained. It is remarkable in comparison how tenuous and insecure the legal relations, with their ceremonials and uniforms, can become. Something of this sort first became clear to me during the civil war[39]—until the mothers join in, revolutions also remain harmless. But then come the moments in which even the best troops simply forget to shoot. Where the women have left the fear of death behind them, things happen with the force of a primordial current.

It can be observed that a sentence like this is also correct at deeper levels, all the way from the infallible choice of words to the position and sequence in which the vocals are arranged. Thus, in its second part, the lament progresses by way of three emphasized vowels down three grand steps. But it is at the beginning that the words ring through most strangely and outrageously, namely, in the secret rejoicing with which the now-inalienable property is taken possession of. The male trajectory is seen like that of a flying fish: emerging from the elements, it plays for

39. Likely a reference to the revolutionary unrest in Berlin, Munich, and elsewhere from the last days of the First World War until the formal establishment of the Weimar Republic in August 1919.

a short moment in the colored light and returns to the depths, returns to the mother.

Postscript ***Überlingen***

Incidentally, I made another particular observation in this matter: when I hear that brothers have been apprehended in these kinds of affairs, the criminal element seems dimmed or weakened. A contributing factor here must be a memory of times in which kinship was decisive in legal questions. But the opposite conception also exists, namely, that the criminal element erupts in a particularly malicious form here, inasmuch as it does not limit itself to the individual but engulfs the whole family—and I gather from court decisions and newspaper commentaries that this is the prevalent conception in our parts. To this corresponded, without a doubt, the procedures of the early royal and priestly civic offices; indeed, wherever families come into conflict with the state, we may surmise places where this taming is still incomplete.

Knowledge of this antithesis may hold a small key, by which an individual can establish more reliably than by any bodily markings whether, and to what degree, he belongs to the primordial race.

Intuitive Skepticism[40] ***Steglitz***

Besides the theoretical skepticism of the philosophers, there exists a more dangerous, intuitive one—a form of insight far removed from the norm, which perhaps only becomes possible because nature does not precisely enough tailor the robes she casts over life. Consequently, all manner of superfluity remains at the seams. For instance, it is superfluous that a fish still jumps around in the red-hot pan after the cook has slaughtered it. Similarly, we continue having superfluous perceptions in situations in which unconsciousness may be preferable, such as during a plummet into the abyss.

Of course, what is superfluous and painful in our natural life may be immeasurably enlightening in our spiritual one. There is also a level of astonishment that drives away fear—in this state, a fine veil that nearly

40. The original title, *Anschaulicher Skeptizismus*, could be equally well rendered, while remaining within the logic of this piece, by "Perceptual Skepticism," in the sense that the perceptions give immediate birth to the skeptical intuition.

always shrouds the world is lifted. Thus it is said that a perfect calm prevails in the eye of the cyclone. Things are supposedly seen more dispassionately, more lucidly and distinctly than otherwise. At points like this, the eye is given access to unauthorized insights, since the exaggerated reality resembles a mirror in which the illusionary is also revealed.

It seems to me that in the war too, immediately after the storming of the first trenches, a similar stillness spread over the field. After the hurricane of the artillery, after the charge and the man-to-man battles, a deep ebb rolled in. The mad raging of the battle at its most intense was displaced by a sudden silence. With the destruction of the adversary, the principle of the proceedings had been fulfilled, but also suspended; and for a short time, the battlefield resembled an ant heap, whose disruption froze it under a spell of meaninglessness. Everyone stood motionless—like spectators before whose eyes a gigantic firework had been let off, but at the same time as the perpetrators of horrendous deeds.

Then the ear began to perceive the monotone cries of the wounded; it seemed that a single enormous explosion had simultaneously struck everyone. A prodigious creaturely suffering was expressed in these cries, which were at the same time a delayed protest of life against the still-fuming historical machinery that had rolled on heedlessly over flesh and blood.

Moments like these are so vivid in my memory that I still seem to taste the odor of the powder that rose in billows from the projectile-ploughed ground. A bizarre expression of bewilderment was written on the faces—as if the perplexing answer to a long puzzled-over riddle had materialized from behind the fiery stage set, which had vanished as if by a stroke of magic. Before the jaded inner eye smoldered the complementary colors of a glowing, flashing mirage that fed on the stupor of the dream and on a fervor verging on madness.

That the world is a giant madhouse, but with method and perhaps wickedness behind the madness - - - that we had participated, as improvising extras under the laws of a higher stage direction, in a spectacle during which we could not think and whose image, frozen before us, we only now gathered into our awareness - - - that we had been on duty in the highest Prussian sense - - - all this was intuited in a state without thought, in a mixture of exhaustion and acumen and with an awareness sharpened by the proximity of death.

Perhaps the world had decked itself out too opulently with the red and yellow tones of fire; now its blackened rafters appeared as an after-image. And yet a light-hearted feeling grazed over us like a fan, similar to the feeling we have on awakening in recalling the entanglements of our dreams.

Had the world spirit perhaps shifted its wrappings a little too vigorously, a little too hastily, so that what had been veiled appeared for a moment to the blunted senses? When the world comes apart at the seams, fissures appear through which we are able to divine architectural secrets normally concealed from us. And so it seemed to me that a deeper reality than that of victory had momentarily seized our hearts, even as the muzzles of death took aim at them anew from the second line.

Scrupulants and Trombonists ***Überlingen***

An inclination to scrupulosity and the microscopic is among the first signs that betray a deterioration of natural health. Our sensory apparatus is set up to deal with people and things in a certain practical manner. When things are in order with us, our pleasures are lively, our grasp is decisive, and our appetites are not too fastidious. Thus the pores in the skin on a human face should generally not be apparent to us.

In a weakened state, on the contrary, the general impression recedes and the details press themselves on us. Intellectual and physical aversions awaken and our senses are sharpened by an incommensurate refinement. Sounds, smells, and colors engage us more easily, and food causes aversion. Above all, meat becomes repugnant, as do tobacco and strong drinks; this repulsion soon extends to our interactions with those enjoying these pleasures. An abstainer's intolerance arises.

The mind shows itself inclined to apprehension, doubt, and hair-splitting. The ulterior and ambiguous emerge more forcefully. By contrast, the interrelationships fade into the background; our intellect comprehends the individual words more readily than the sentences and framework. This gives rise to an intricate, punctuated form of antagonism, which disrupts the flow of the proceedings. In writing, an exaggerated purity is the result; thought aspires to ever more refined forms, grammatical scruples begin to curb the free flow of ideas, and this can even escalate to subtle game-playing. The result is a strained style, which at times mystifies through its arid beauty and artificial health—prose for vegetarians. It corresponds to an empty classicism in the fine arts.

Another part of this picture is a kind of sensitivity that is able to examine moral qualities as if through a magnifying glass: the morbid acuity of someone with a spoiled appetite for humanity. Secret incongruities then surface in the faces, laughter becomes objectionable, and the tone of voice openly betrays the ploys and intentions motivating the speaker. This delicacy of feeling readily extends to reflexive observations, for instance in the scrupulous confessor, a type not lacking in Protestant lands either.

Corresponding to the category of the scrupulant, who measures everything with the most delicate weights, is another who only handles colossal loads and whom we can call the trombonist. This second breed might be even more questionable, because whereas a speck of dust still comprises at least a tiny bit of earth, in the second case the totally indeterminate element of air reigns. Here things take on a windy, blown-up character, become lopsided and distended. They swing back and forth like a weathercock in a storm of moods and opinions.

Whereas scrupulants will be found to incline toward pessimism, trombonists generally tend to optimism. The one has something sedentary and withdrawn about it, the other something agitated and erratic. Here the mind drills like a watchmaker into ever-finer casings, while there it puffs out a series of changing shapes with powerful blasts. Here we see the concentrically active mind, there the eccentrically active one. The first likes to wrap itself up in sectarian relationships, the other loves big gatherings and the open market. By following a trombonist over the years, a catalogue of his inclinations could be compiled—for example, as a philosopher, he blows his way through complete systems.

When he visits, the trombonist can be heard down in the hallway; he steps briskly into the room and immediately seizes the conversation. If he encounters resistance, he clears out, disgruntled. But his grudge is short-lived, for his appearance repeats itself a couple of times a year. The views he got excited about last time may have since been exposed in their full windiness. But it would be futile to point this out to him, since he lacks intellectual shame and consequently a continuous sense of responsibility.

The scrupulant by contrast slips in quietly, preferably at twilight. His subtle and unusual way of seeing things is often initially surprising. Soon enough however the deformity appears like a horse's hoof; he requires that we acquiesce to some or other nonsense. If he finds us unwilling, he excuses himself with pointed phrases and is never seen again. Nevertheless, he and his ilk are heard from later, because spirits like these often enjoy sect-building power.

These are the two deviations we mostly come into contact with. They resemble concave and convex mirrors, each of which distorts the picture in its own sense. Sometimes it appears that nothing is more rare than a healthy, practical mind. But only it is capable of putting things on the right track. The countless blows that land nearby do not drive in the nail, only the one that hits the mark.

Beach Passages (3) ***Helgoland***

During my first circuit of the uplands, I was taken by surprise near the North Cape by a raucous, many-voiced clamor; it reminded me that one of the particularities of this island was its summer colony of northern murres.

A moment later, I saw the birds setting out from the cliffs; their nesting sites were hidden from view by the overhanging bluffs. Only the birds whizzing to and fro were visible; they soared as straight as arrows to their breeding spots, like bees to an immense hive, and then turned back from there to their fishing grounds. I tried in vain to follow them with my gaze; they flew far out to sea and disappeared as points in the endlessness. In the same way, the returning birds reappeared out of the emptiness of the horizon.

The spectacle possessed a bewitching orderliness, whose sight called forth a state of mental bedazzlement. The sea assumed the aspect of a gleaming disc, from whose circumference the winged creatures streamed together like rays toward a hidden midpoint, only to disperse back in the same formation. The soporific sheen of this mirror appeared further heightened by the fine network of flight paths laid out over it like a strictly delineated grid.

Figures like this at the same time call forth a special refinement or crystallization of the eye; like double-ground lenses, they seem to confer greater acuity to our sight. In their telluric mathematics, they present a mighty spectacle, in which the powers and orders of the earth are exhibited more openly than usual. As in the second canto of the *Messiah*, there is also a tone of terror blended with the triumph in these visions—as if a tremendously restrained power stirred before us. But above all we sense something familiar sounding in them, like a primordial melody—the bold double-dealing of the spirit, which so strongly engages us and is yet so deeply concealed from us. On the one hand, this game aspires to a supreme, metallic resolution of consciousness; on the other, it loses itself in the wild zones of elemental forces.

In these two tendencies, which so differ from one another and even seem to contradict each other like dream and reality, are hidden the unity and multiplicity of our so mysterious world. We encounter them in every important issue of our times, in each of its theories and significant phenomena, indeed in the character of every individual of distinction. Nothing characterizes us better than this coexistence of tremendous, unchained power with an unflinching boldness of view—this is our style, one of volcanic precision, whose uniqueness will perhaps only be recognized after us.

Nonetheless, there are things that historical consciousness will scarcely be able to reconstruct, such as the wild and fortuitous manner in which the elemental and orderly aspects of our powers alternate like fire and ice. We navigate this world as through a titanic city, here lit up by the glow of dreadful conflagrations, while there workers lay down the foundations of an immense construction. Images of a deep, dull suffering that seems to be happening in a dream alternate in rapid succession with the demonic invulnerability of the spirit that subjects the chaos to the spell of its lights and lightning bolts and its crystalline figures.

But just as the image of the sea's surface is united here with the astute movements of the insect-like birds, so places may be imagined in which these two great motifs approach each other and fuse; and it is possible that the metaphysical part of our mission lies in this conjunction.

On Désinvolture — *Goslar*

Things whose absence no one even notices are not among the worst things. One of these is *désinvolture*, a way of being for which we lack an adequate expression. One usually sees the word translated as "nonchalant";[41] inasmuch as this indicates straightforward conduct, it is

41. The original, *Ungeniertheit*, could also be translated as unabashed, uninhibited, artless, free and easy, or unceremonious.

correct. However, another meaning is simultaneously concealed in the word, referring to a godlike superiority. I understand *désinvolture* in this sense as the innocence of power.

Wherever *désinvolture* is intact, there can be no doubt concerning questions of power. It must have still been visible in Louis XIV when he dissolved Parliament. This occurred to me while contemplating Bernini's bust of him in Versailles; yet a certain posturing had already come into the picture there. In this order, the sovereigns are so unassailable that even revolts are led in their names. On the other hand, when *désinvolture* disappears, the mighty begin moving as men off-balance; they cling to the subordinate guiding principle of virtue. This is a sure sign of imminent downfall. I believe the characters of Louis XV or Friedrich Wilhelm II, whose portrait by Anton Graff provides first-rate clues, provide subtle insights in this regard. "After us, the flood"—there is a second hidden meaning here. As the last in line, one partakes of a certain fortune, but leaves no heir behind. All will be squandered.

A confident command over princely riches is also a matter of *désinvolture*. Men can look without envy at gold when it lies in a noble palm. Seeing the lucky Aladdin enthroned in his palace, the poor porter praises Allah who bestows such great gifts. In our own times, wealth elicits a guilty conscience in men, who then try to justify themselves through virtue. In the midst of their affluence, they do not seek to live like wealthy patrons but rather petty bookkeepers.

Désinvolture lies in one's make-up, as a gift, and as such it is more closely related to luck or magic than to the will. Our ideas of power have long been distorted by an exaggerated connection to will. The city tyrants of the Renaissance are modest examples, technicians of lesser rank. Man is certainly a little more than merely a predator—he is the king of the predators. Here it occurs to me that the knight in the lion's den also possesses *désinvolture*.

On a banquet table around which many guests are gathered, a golden apple is displayed, which no one dares touch. Everyone has a burning wish to possess it but feels that a terrible uproar would ensue if he even hinted at the desire. Then a child walks into the hall and casually grabs the apple; a deep, happy consent fills the guests.

As the irresistible grace of power, *désinvolture* is a particular form of serenity—of course, this word needs rehabilitation, like so many in our language. Serenity is among the most powerful weapons at man's disposal—he wears it as divine armor, in which he can withstand even the terrors of annihilation. And from this luminous force that dissolves into the morning dew of history, *désinvolture* still reaches deep into reckoned time, like a scion raised in a noble house. When it appears, it is their very own myth that takes hold of the people.

This order of things can also be recalled architecturally. Thus there is only one building here in Goslar that is a worthy setting for *désinvolture*. It is not the badly reconstructed Imperial Palatinate, but rather the old Town Hall by the market, a jewel sculpted in gray stone. Observed from the fountain side, one sees in its simultaneously light yet powerfully extended arches a portal worthy of princes.

Postscript to Désinvolture — *Überlingen*

An idea I periodically come back to is that of an unchanging landscape that exists within the changing epochs, one in which the spiritual circumstances are visible. Corresponding to this, there must be a way of interpreting the philosophical positions as if one were reading travel journals. One can establish the latitudes at which the author found himself, the islands and coasts along which he traveled. But there are also capes or landmarks that cannot be discovered by thought but which must have actually been seen. In regard to *désinvolture*, such a place just caught my eye in my readings, specifically in Bacon's *Essays*:

> Overt and apparent virtues, bring forth praise; but there be secret and hidden virtues, that bring forth fortune; certain deliveries of a man's self, which have no name. The Spanish name 'desenvoltura' partly expresseth them; when there be not stonds nor restiveness in a man's nature; but that the wheels of his mind, keep way with the wheels of his fortune.[42]

This passage occurs in a treatise on fortune, which distinguishes itself by other remarkable sentences; for instance, that there are no two more fortunate characteristics than to possess something of the fool and not too much of the honest man. This is one of those remarks by which an author demonstrates his mastery over language. Incidentally, Bacon's

42. From Bacon's "Of Fortune," in *Essays or Counsels, Civil and Moral, of Francis Ld. Verulam, Viscount St. Albans*, no. 40 (Mount Vernon, NY: Peter Pauper, 1963), p. 158.

language is particularly well suited to treatment of these matters, insofar as the blossoms of our expressions lie yet in the bud there.

Historia in Nuce: The Lost Position — *Goslar*

One particular figure of our destiny may be characterized as that of the lost position—and no one knows if just this destiny will not someday be visited on him. There are times when fate approaches with haste, like a bank of fog that surprises us in the high mountains. In other cases, we see the danger approaching from afar; in confronting it, we are like a chess player preparing himself for a long, shrewd endgame, even though he recognizes the inevitability of defeat.

Even when calamity forces smaller or larger groups into lost positions, there is an overnight awakening, above all wherever history works through its hidden channels. We tend to believe that the catastrophe announces itself from afar and that conspicuous signs precede it. Far more commonly, however, a historical building is undermined by the burrowing of ants. Then the mere breath from the utterance of a word can bring it down. Terror marches smartly in where moments before the guests were still celebrating around the banquet table. As they jump to their feet, these life-boozers recognize in the light of the flames the illusion with which security mystifies man.

All the signs of this state of affairs become plainly visible when time is allowed to ripen them. This can happen in very different ways. Cities of believers can long survive in countries in which alien sacrifices are already being offered all around them, for instance in the Acre of the Templars or in Moorish Grenada. In the same way, establishments like schools, monasteries, or foreign trading posts can often live on for decades in isolation. In one's own land, the same thing can happen to communities, classes, or families. In the midst of persecution, islands survive, which the terror long overlooks; this is how Rivarol[43] lived in Paris.

In such circumstances, life often becomes lucid and transparent to a previously unknown degree. Just as we see the stars most clearly from our observatories erected on firn ice, so our own constellations become

43. Antoine Comte de Rivarol (1753–1801), a French writer and *philosophe* known for his contempt for the French Revolution. Jünger clearly identified with Rivarol, translating his work and composing a lengthy essay on him in the mid-1950s.

clearer in lost positions. Even the habitual and everyday gains special dignity, a higher rank. This first became apparent to me after our retreat from the Somme in making a round of the evacuated positions. Each of our actions contains an essence that is unknown to us.

In coming face-to-face with annihilation, these characteristics emerge in their most visible form. A man then no longer acts in accordance with his self-preservation but rather with his meaning. Thus, the death of the last defenders follows the downfall of famed old cities such as Carthage, Sagunt, or Zion like a pure show sacrifice. At that point, the individual no longer discharges the duties of his particular post but rather those of a sacral witness who is to meet his death at the consecrated place, be it on the city walls, before the statues, or on the steps of the highest temple. The same sequence of events takes place on the deck of a sinking warship, in which is represented the invulnerability of the native earth. In such situations, a man is capable of the subtlest distinctions, even if he has never considered them before. And so he knows that it is permissible to be picked out of the water by his conqueror, but not off the sinking ship. He may also hope that if he can withstand up to a certain point, higher powers will take him on board. A dignified kind of joy, stronger than that of love, surprises the warrior in the face of death. It is the source of the banter in Etzel's[44] thirsty feast hall, under the Icelandic palace's burning roof.

With such spectacles, history takes its highest pictorial form, in the very center of time. A sublime sense of enacting something final and definitive can take hold of a man here, a feeling whose light is essential to every good portrayal of the Last Supper. A similar mood illuminates life in isolated and doomed regions, in the great plagues as well. The plague chronicles of St. Gallen show its signs—an autumnal mixture of sadness and joy, a feeling of spiritual brotherhood and the symbolic nature of the actions. Not to be forgotten in this connection is also the last gathering of the threatened family, as vile blood-hate inflames the city. Here, deep beneath the surface of social contracts, the power of a man's alliances first becomes apparent to him.

In lost positions, life is forced into choices, just as matter under high pressure reveals its crystalline forms. That which is base also emerges

44. King Etzel of the Huns (Attila the Hun), from the *Nibelungenlied*.

more plainly, for instance in the wild debauchery of a pirate crew on the deck of their sinking ship. Accordingly, individuals in organizations are prepared in advance for the crisis, during which they are to stand their ground, as if the last man, without orders and companions. The rank of such representations is recognizable by their formation of centers around which the whole action orients itself, even in the heart of dissolution. The representative power of the individual can be tremendous; history provides us with examples of how a single honest witness turned a verdict around, though the millions remained silent.

Historical studies are accordingly among the intellectual instruments that are indispensable to a higher understanding of the world. A voice rings out from the great encounters between men that have been depicted for us by tradition, and it is directed at us too; our archives contain unsurpassable answers to the question of how to act in lost positions. Among the great teachings that are concealed in history, like in a secret school, is that of learning to die. In this sense, Louis XVI did the right thing during his imprisonment in the temple by occupying himself with the history of Charles I.

The Picture Puzzle ***Überlingen***

Nigromontanus's endearing melancholy—that of a gardener working in endangered gardens far from the palace. This characteristic may have been related to his profession, since he always sought out higher grades of solitude and an undivided perspective on matters.

As such, he was born to teach, as a bird is to fly; and it astounded me more and more profoundly how unobtrusively he was able to guide me into his domain. As a child learning arithmetic is at first given a wire frame with red and white balls to play with, so his guidelines were materially based; he had antechambers, in which his mode of thinking was oriented to the tangible. In his view, thinking was a craft; he maintained that it should be practiced on matter, and he adored his materially tinged synonyms. He also did not speak of his students, but of his apprentices.

His first lesson was instruction in seeing, which he gave as occasions arose during informal conversation. He allowed an uninhibited flight here, as long as it proceeded from point to point—that is, his only correction was to continually refer the abstract back to the object. The moment his partner got lost in pure thought or feeling, he would bring the conversation back around with an inconspicuous turn of the hand, like threading a needle.

In the first year, he dealt only with the teaching of surfaces. Like all words, this one also had special meaning for him—he even considered light and mind surfaces that matter could generate. He taught of our intimate fraternity with all things ephemeral and mobile, but also of the art of separating from them at the right moment—he thus revered the snake as his totemic animal. And quite in contrast to all that we hear in the higher schools, he taught us to trust the senses, which he called testimonies of a Golden Age, just as islands are testimonies of sunken continents. He said that surfaces always hide insights in their colorful patterns—just as the presence of hidden water or ore deposits can be surmised from the herbs and flowers growing on the surface. The investigation of these contacts of the sensory world with deeper currents was to be included among the illuminating exercises. He maintained that we examine visible things far too cursorily, which perhaps explained his fondness for surrounding himself with objects that transformed in curious ways on closer observation.

He thus loved mutably colored fabrics, as well as iridescent glass and liquids, whose colors shimmered or changed with the light. His favorite stones were the opal and polished tourmaline. He also had a collection of disguised pictures that emerged magically from monochromatic mosaics. These were composed of something like little stones, indistinguishable in daylight from other similarly grained ones, but which lit up phosphorically with the twilight. Sometimes he could be seen sitting by a stove on which sayings in red script appeared when it was heated, or on a garden terrace where a rain shower conjured up black symbols. So too the decorations in his rooms and on his apparatuses disclosed unexpected things to the eye: a meander on which a dark stream and its light banks alternately came to the fore, and a dice drawn on the flat plane, which at one moment turned its front to the viewer, at the next its underside. He also had transparent foils on which harmless things turned into horrible ones or something terrifying became beautiful when light was shone through them. He loved kaleidoscopes and had some made for himself in which polished semi-precious stones composed themselves with the elegance of thought into rosettes and stars, in which freedom and symmetry vied with each other. I often delighted myself with them in the garden house he had built outside the gates of Wolfenbüttel, a small but significant country town. On Saturdays, we would make our way there to examine old manuscripts, and he occasionally ran into fantastical acquaintances from far-away places.

In thinking back on the objects that amused me during these diversions, it appears that Nigromontanus gathered them around himself according to a definite principle—that of the picture puzzle. Through the accumulation of such objects, he undoubtedly wanted to evoke specific effects. Incidentally, this was not limited to tangible objects; he also appreciated the enigmatic power in writing, and he occasionally put a book in my hand whose prose had to be followed like an animal spoor that led past wolves' dens. Others were presented differently again, let us say like a painted ceiling through whose openings heavenly bodies could be glimpsed: for example, a wonderful *ineditum* on the Eleusinian Mysteries that had passed down to him from the secret legacy of Fiorelli. Like other of his inclinations, this rubbed off on me—I adopted from him a partiality for the secret correspondences existing between things.

With his picture puzzles, he aimed above all at the moment of shock that seizes us when we unexpectedly see in one thing quite another. Perhaps he intended thereby to loosen and tear through the fine roots that bind our being to our everyday routine. He was right in this—when we solve a picture puzzle, bewilderment, astonishment, fright, but also exhilaration can result. When such impressions accumulate, we start approaching things differently; now we observe even the simple building blocks of our conceptions with attention, expectation, or even suspicion. This was precisely what Nigromontanus intended; his methodology was disposed not to searching, as it was in the higher schools, but to finding. He was characterized by a faith that a special result lay in each of our passages, like a kernel in a nut, even in the seemingly aimless and fruitless ones; and he required that we crack open the day's memories like a shell before going to sleep.

Such exercises were intended to show that even the world in a greater sense is composed like a picture puzzle—that its secrets lie exposed on the surface and that only a minimal adjustment of the eye is required to view its wealth of treasures and wonders. He loved citing Hesiod's saying that the gods conceal mankind's sustenance from them and that a day's labor should suffice for a whole year's harvest. So too a moment's reflection should be enough to discover the key to treasure chambers sufficient for a lifetime—to illustrate this, he pointed out those simple inventions that everyone would afterward say had been child's play to work out. He also liked referring to fantasy: its fertility was an analogy of a universal fertility; yet mankind lived as one dying of thirst in the midst of inexhaustible water springs. He said at one point that the world had been given to us in its elements like the twenty-six letters of the alphabet—and that the elaboration of its image depended on the texts we wrote. Naturally, one had to be a genuine author and not merely a scribe.

He came to speak of this as I accompanied him on one of his geomantic walks at the edge of the Harz Mountains, along that mysterious stretch where the old watchtowers had been erected. He used the occasion to express perhaps most clearly of all what he intended by methodology. If I have it correct, he understood it as the art of living, with the everlasting as the goal. This lifestyle conformed to the true image of the world, which was laid out within ordinary life like a picture puzzle—so close as to be inapprehensible. Astonishment, followed by exhilaration, were the first signs of a successful sighting of it.

In remembering all this, it seems that I was not in the proper state for these teachings. Yes, I did experience the wonderful agitation that overcomes us when the boundaries are obliterated and hidden meanings emerge—but only like someone flying over exotic gardens. And so I took part in life like in the big game at the moment one's luck arrives; yet Nigromontanus had taught me the art by which one always wins, whether in a hermit's cell or at a palace ball.

The Green Woodpecker — *Überlingen*

During my first walks here, I had the impression that the landscape was imbued with an unusual liveliness. This must be due to the concert of the countless birds that inhabit the surface and shores of the lake. The less distinct and more finely diffused such impressions are, the deeper they penetrate—there exists such a thing as an ether of gaiety.

This richness of feathered life, that even extends to a broad band of the gardens and vineyard slopes around the lakeshore, is clearly due to the meticulous, almost park-like cultivation of the loose and extensive stands of fruit trees that cover the land. The advantages of the forest and the plains come together in open groves like these; their winged visitors find a favorable medium that provides abundant opportunity for free flight as well as for cover.

The most charming images present themselves to the eye—fields that seem to be covered with a luminous yellow gauze of yellowhammers, or old pear-tree trunks on which dainty tree creepers, mouse-like nut-hatches, and lots of colorful chickadees are all busy at the same time. Even the predatory birds turn up in flocks; this explains the disused wine barrels in the farmsteads with small doors cut out to provide a quick refuge for the chicks.

There are also lots of green woodpeckers flying back and forth; their mocking laughter is heard from near and far. Though I have often observed them during my life, their essential nature, indeed that of woodpeckers in general, has only now become clear to me. We have to do here with a creature that must have occupied a peculiar position during creation, to be precise, the point where the dividing line between rhythm and melos was most sharply drawn. In this manner, a first-class rhythm player was created, one so gifted that no room remained in it for melody.

The metered and starkly accentuated nature of its movements is thus immediately noticeable in any activity the green woodpecker is busy with. Even in its approach, its distinctive rising and dipping flight is unmistakable; no other bird traces out such a wave-like flight pattern. This matches the jumpy way the bird spirals around or springs up tree trunks, as well as the time-beating bobbing of its head. There is also its unmelodious call, a whinnying, drawn-out whistle with numerous uniform pauses notched into it. The final, most characteristic part of this picture is the well-known hammering and tapping with which it fills the woods; in the great symphony of the birds, the woodpeckers chose the drums.

Those aware of the relationship between rhythm and the limbs, in particular the hands, will also find interesting the paired opposition of the toes, the front pair of which are fused. The structure of the tongue is equally remarkable, and even in the gaudy, harshly contrasted coloration of the plumage, the absence of any harmonious basic substance is apparent.

This analysis could be extended right into the particulars; indeed, these kinds of relationships become increasingly more apparent to me than Darwin's observations, on the woodpecker's red crest for instance. Yet for me the value of these combinations lies in an altogether different field—they are in fact of a more general, or better, of a more disclosing nature: small models of another way of seeing things. It strikes me that our education system has failed here in all the decisive points, indeed in even approaching them, and that it only continues to deteriorate. In this respect, we should be grateful to the early natural scientists for having, at least in some measure, pursued a theological focus in parallel as a minor field; they had a point of contact there, which connected at any rate better than that of the actual theologians. Today, anyone wanting to really work, that is to say, to advance into the no man's land of thought, must first, in order to even begin, acquire the tools of the trade of every faculty. Nietzsche was thus correct in saying that, in regard to higher ambitions, one is still a child today, still a beginner, at thirty—and even at forty, yet only an apprentice.

Courage and Audacity[45] — *On Board*

In the course of our lives, we leave certain moltings behind us in regard to language as well. Here it occurs to me that in the last years I have increasingly lost my taste for certain words combined with *super*.[46] I do not intend constructions like *surplus*,[47] which subsist under the sign of the cornucopia, but rather those whose tone is given by the will.

When things get really dangerous, the intensifiers soon abandon us, and when the ground quakes, we have no desire to talk in lofty tones. Courage[48] is such an elevated virtue that it needs none of the enhancement that is inherent in praises of audacity.[49] The notions of impulsive, full-blooded, muscular characters that step triumphantly onto the battlefield of life are born from the covetous dreams of the consumptive.

The common misconception here lies in the fact that such a flourishing condition deters rather than encourages supreme exertions. It fails

45. *Mut und Übermut*.

46. Or *sur-*. In the original, *über*, as in the title.

47. *Überfluss* in the original.

48. *Mut* in the original.

49. *Über-Mut* in the original—"super-courage." Unfortunately there is no English word with this meaning that also uses the prefix *super-* or *sur-*. Audacity comes closest to Jünger's meaning of the word and is used in the remainder of the passage.

to recognize that we usually only come eye to eye with the real decisions when our life forces are beginning to expire. We reach the arena as troops already utterly exhausted by interminable marches, hunger, thirst, night watches, and outpost skirmishes, for whom the greatest demand still lies ahead, that of victory. This relationship is plainly reflected in life itself—death only approaches when sickness, loss of blood, or violence has preceded it. At these crossroads, audacity quickly melts away.

It should also be remembered that audacity has above all a mobile, aggressive character—and so to avoid being ridiculous, one must perforce be the stronger party. But the essential core of courage is undoubtedly of a quiet nature and can be discerned in traits like persistence, steadiness, and unshakableness. Given this constitution, courage also surfaces in the face of the highest dangers, for instance against an overwhelming superiority.

The strict order by which the process unfolds when a confrontation takes place under these conditions is astonishing. If the conflict is maintained at an exemplary level, the confrontation is preceded under all circumstances by an act of the superior force, namely, a demand to surrender. As diverse the forms this demand may take, the differences are irrelevant. The general expects the little captain whose fort lies on his path of advance to give himself up honorably as a prisoner of war. The cunning tyrant is satisfied with a bow, while his minions are accustomed to having their victims kiss the dirt at their feet. Surrender can also take place almost invisibly, for instance through an observation of silence, or by the acceptance of war proceeds or tributes. There are many kinds of nooses, some even graciously veiled, but all tighten in the same way. The real business becomes instantly apparent when there is any hesitation. Then the call becomes increasingly urgent, quickly escalating to a threat of deadly, annihilating violence.

In sensing this menace, the spirit is gripped by a moment of weakness, which scarcely one in a thousand can withstand. But if a man overcomes this spell, an uncommon act takes place—he becomes oriented to the impossible. There is no outcome here, no matter how distant, on which the eye can fix; like the intersection of the parallels, the focal point is at infinity. With this act, the battle enters a new order. A man becomes less subject to gravity and thereby gains new powers. The influx is like a surge that rushes in after the lowest tide, as over a lowered weir. This marvelous invigoration confers a terrifying might even to the weak; it arms them with the power of spirits.

Of course, there is no victory recipe for the underdog hidden in these relations. Far more, they concern forces whose manifestation confirms the world order, in itself and in its essence, though almost always without success on the plane of time. In this manner, the national hero towers up in the destiny of his people: appearing in dark times, unrecognized throughout his life, often sold out to the enemy, and always ending in lonely demise. Nevertheless, time and again the moments recur in which an example and a sacrificial victim are required to restore the measure by which man has been created and cultivated. This is signified in every great hierarchy; for our ancestors, the unchanging paradigm was thus not the prince's victory on the battlefield, but the glorious deeds of the dead—a wonderfully concise formula that immediately and decisively confronts anyone with an inclination to distinguish themselves.

In the Museums ***Überlingen***

There is always something enthralling and even frightening about museum visits. Now and then we are also witnesses to poignant characters there—for instance, that of the atheistic freethinker standing before an archaeopteryx footprint as if before an unveiled relic. Unfortunately, we do not have expressions at our disposal adequate to represent such observations; otherwise, journeys like Pausanias's second-century visit to the antiquities would certainly have provided us with rich spoils. We do not understand the shiver that runs over us when astronomers talk to us in light-year figures or archaeologists resurrect the city gates of an unknown metropolis from the rubble of millennia.

We also easily underestimate the power and extension that the museum impulse has gained and daily continues to gain. We get an idea of the formidable appetite reigning here when we consider how churches are transforming into museums. Innumerable people today visit them as nothing more than museums, and the churches adapt accordingly. Their personnel can also not be shielded from the zeitgeist; the line between custodian and sexton blurs imperceptibly. Corresponding to this, among other things, is a remarkable transformation of relics from sacred objects into museum exhibits. Hence the Reichenau Museum here has a tankard of great antiquity on exhibition, which through the centuries no one at all doubted had been used at the marriage of Cana. Today this is mentioned as a curiosity; the reverence expected in its regard resembles, if anything, that awaiting the owner of a Ming Dynasty vase. Like all things, this transformation, which often calls for a fine eye, has a political flip side. In museum matters, church and state meet today in a common foyer. Situations arise in which the Leviathan could swallow all that remains in the aftermath of secularization in one bite, were it not held back by a certain wariness. In reality, a seamless solution spares it some inconveniences, and so a far more cunning arrangement than could be achieved by partition or even force lies in granting the clergy a sort of custodial position. As a keeper of antiquities, be they buildings and artworks or customs and conventions, the church gets involved in a peculiar business, whose novelty is its museum character. This novelty is in turn only the contemporary expression of a repeating constellation—travelers to cities of antiquity also visited half-forgotten temples and were shown age-old things there, such as holy tripods fallen from the heavens.

Incidentally, we not infrequently see the old families entering into similar arrangements. These days we encounter not only princes who are barely distinguishable in their family castles from museum directors, but also others whose income is derived from the entrance fees and consumption of the masses of converging visitors. It is in such places that one first gains a true sense of the power of democracy. It presses a tip into the milord's palm.

This much regards zones that the museum impulse only occupies as a minor field. It is above all in the field of natural and historical conservation that it establishes a taboo entity of the greatest dimension; a growing abundance of objects are sheltered under its stewardship, from tiny insects to national parks as large as whole states. Today there are flowers, trees, forests, moors, houses, villages, cities, and peoples upon which a museum taboo lies, and even the keenest imagination cannot judge the goal that this impulse must be aiming at in order to draw such masses of living and dead things into the untouchable zone.

Remarkable too is the direct coexistence of this world tucked under a glass bell with another in which riotous barbarism and broad swathes of destruction barely still know limits. Yet these two exist in a secret interrelationship, inasmuch as consciousness triumphs in overpowering fashion over the residues of conservative and senatorial forms. In this sense, the museum impulse may represent a safeguard that civilization splits off from itself. It thereby creates an artificial counterbalance to its commercial and technical devastation, one that in cases like the native Americans or African big game at least often prevents complete extinction. This practice can take on grandiose forms by shielding broad regions from full irradiation by abstract consciousness, be they landscapes, crafts, or even nationalities enclosed in larger entities. We often find a barely separable blending of conservative and conservational efforts here, though there can be no doubting the unity of the underlying process.

Perhaps we generally do well to turn our focus away from the intentions and instead observe the figures as though nature or some obscure instinct had brought them forth; above all, we should never allow ourselves to rely on the explanations that contemporary man tries to provide for his efforts. In this perspective, the kinship existing between our museum kingdom and the great cults of graves and the dead becomes apparent, and it would become even clearer were we to lay out parts of the collections in underground spaces. The death side of science is revealed in the museum impulse—an inclination to embed life into the dormant and invulnerable, perhaps also to compile an enormous and painstakingly ordered material catalogue that leaves behind a faithful effigy of our life and its most obscure stirrings. We may be reminded of the contents of Tutankhamen's grave.

Where science unites with the museum impulse, it averts its focus from the will, and the mistrust that fills its technically oriented branches disappears therewith; neither patents nor fear of spies exist here. And however much the unpleasantness of travel may have increased, exchanges and transactions in the museum sphere have at least been assured; everywhere we encounter similar working principles and dispositions, a state of affairs otherwise characteristic only of the buildings of spiritual orders, once scattered widely over lands and kingdoms. In a world where people only too readily cut each other's throats in disputes about the social contract, there are places that remain as untouched by all this as the Oasis of Jupiter Ammon.

By the way, museums additionally share with graves a virtual immunity to critique, as can be easily perceived in the demeanors and on the faces of their visitors. A mighty force resides in the will to endure; we can sense this physically when holding an object in our hands that has been under human care for millennia, above all when it is one of the masterpieces in which the arts culminate. In this sense, the great collections are citadels of the power of conviction, and, insofar as they present a pure crystallization of the human social condition, of high bridging and conservational importance.

These relationships also clearly emerge in the negative stamp: where things have flourished to an extreme and those otherwise deeply suppressed powers are liberated that are not opposed to this or that form of order, but to order as such. During such disruptions, not only are the jails and physical fortresses soon broken open, but the libraries and collections that the mob correctly views as safeguards of culture are also burned down. Indiscriminate iconoclasm is always a sign that the foundations are shaking. In this connection, we will come across very definite indications here that the yeast has started to foam. Among these is the veneration of fire, not in its illuminating but rather in its burning quality, and so appearing through the ages variously as the torch, as petroleum, or as dynamite. An unmistakable indication of this stage are reports that graves have been broken open and their corpses displayed in the public squares. These exhibitions are not merely dark capriccios by which excesses of the human spirit are satisfied, but rather a challenge issued to the human spirit as a whole—because the very basis of the human condition is burial of the dead, and whoever begins to joke around in this context will surely stop at nothing. Consequently, the effect of these spectacles cannot be represented strongly enough; they dissolve the last resistance like a dark whirlpool sucking down into terrible depths. Yet it may sometimes appear that even responsible spirits—a Burckhardt or a Winckelmann, for instance—overestimate the importance of preserving the great works and that this overestimation itself perhaps masks an obscure pain or secret lack of creative power. On the other hand, it can be observed that it is precisely the bad painter, particularly the pretender or the forger, who unites with the mob in their hatred of the great collections; beauty must disappear from the world, so that the ugly becomes passable. Generally speaking, such a powerful phenomenon as this conserving and collecting impulse resists an unequivocal explanation; it is one of the great themes, in which contradictory things unite, as the depths and surfaces of a single landscape.

And so, to keep the best for last, our museum impulse certainly also has a noble side, and that is where it touches on research, which is intimately bound up with collecting. The spark of life lies here, glowing through the dust—our great, exalted inquiry into the riddle of this world. Even the most distant and bygone of things allow us no peace, and our telescopes directed at the stars, our nets plunged into the deep ocean, our trowels that clear away the rubble over lost cities, theaters, and temples—all are moved by the question: if then and there that innermost nucleus of life, the divine power that also moves us, can likewise be detected. And the more extraordinary and mysterious the places from which the answer sounds back to us, be it as the faintest echo over vast expanses of ice and countless millennia, the more deeply will we be delighted.

At the Customs Station — *Überlingen*

Death is like a foreign continent, about which none who tread its ground will report back. Its secrets engage us so intensely that its shadows darken the path that leads to it—that is, we do not distinguish sharply enough between death and dying. The distinction is important, in that much of what we ascribe to death has already been completed in dying, as our glance and imagination still probe now and again into the intermediary zone. As distant as death might still lie, we can already taste the climate surrounding it.

There are also cases that teeter on a razor's edge, where the subject already senses death lying like a reef behind the near breakers. Then life returns into him, as flames reawaken in an almost cold hearth. Such cases resemble a false alarm; and like the captain who only comes to the bridge when a storm threatens, so here an otherwise hidden authority appears and makes its preparations. Man possesses capacities that he carries around with him like sealed documents; he does not make use of them until they are needed. One of these is his ability to comprehend his situation—this is in fact the case here: a moment's bewilderment, then realization precedes the approach of death.

As we cool his brow, the dying person is already infinitely distant from us, whiling in landscapes that are first revealed once his spirit has traversed the flaming curtains of his agony. Time and space, the two germ-leafs from within which life blooms, fold back in on themselves; and in this dwindling away of the external environment, the inner eye gains new perspective.

Life now appears to our subject with new significance, more distant and distinct than otherwise. He is able to survey it like a region on a map; and its development, which stretched over many years, is visible in its essence like lines on the hand. He comprehends his transformation from the perspective of necessity, for the first time without light and shadow. Now it is less the images than their essential content that surfaces, as if, after the opera and the lowering of the curtain, the main theme was played again in the empty space by an invisible orchestra, lonesome, tragic, proud, and with deadly significance. Freed from the compulsion of self-preservation, our man understands a new way of loving his life; and his thoughts gain sovereignty as they extricate themselves from the fears that clouded and weighed down his every thought and judgment.

The question of immortality, so deeply disturbing to the spirit during life, is already resolved at this stage. The solution is extraordinary in that the dying man reaches a point like on a mountain ridge, from which he is able to look into the territories of both life and death—and he gains full assurance by perceiving himself as much in the one as in the other. He experiences a pause in his journey, like at a lonely customs station high in the mountains, where the local coins of his memories are exchanged for gold. His consciousness reaches forward like a light, and by its radiance he recognizes that he is not being cheated, but rather that he is exchanging fear for certainty.

Within this space, which belongs to time and yet already does not, we may also imagine the regions described by religious sects as purgatories. This is the path on which human dignity is restored. No life has been entirely shielded from baseness; none has escaped without loss. But now, in the narrow mountain pass, neither evasion nor hesitation is possible, whatever obstacles loom up. Death determines each step now, as a distant cataract controls the river's flow. On this lonely march that nothing can hinder, a man resembles a soldier winning back his position.

As a child is provided with organs to facilitate and allow birth, so man also possesses organs for death, the formation and strengthening of which belong to theological practices. Where this knowledge is extinguished, a form of idiocy spreads with respect to death; this reveals itself in an escalation of blind fear, but also in an equally blind and mechanical disdain for death.

The Redstart ***Überlingen***

While breakfasting in the garden, I saw a baby bird fall from the redstart nest over my threshold and end up dead on the stone floor. Its body was still naked, and its large eyeballs shone darkly through the pink skin. These and the wide, tightly shut beak lent the little corpse a painful, precocious character.

The abrupt plummet from safety into the void was that much more poignant because in the same moment the little creature disappeared without a trace from its parents' perception. They continued flying faithfully to and from their little nest with food for the remaining siblings, often passing close by the little dead body without a trace of interest.

I have often made the observation that animals are equipped with a different, indeed a sharper perception of the living than we are. Death very quickly transforms a body for them into an object; there are examples in which the parents immediately perceive the corpse of their young in its nutritional aspect. Animals thereby abide most decisively by Heraclitus's maxim on the corpse, which it describes as refuse, and that I assume was directed against the Egyptian cult of the dead. It seems that animals grasp themselves not as images, but rather as manifestations of life—we can visualize this relationship like our own to an electric lamp that illuminates us because, and only as long as, there is current in it.

The little incident led me to a consideration that I find a happy one, namely, that a common spirit is developed in the nest in a manner that surpasses our imagination. Individuation is correspondingly undeveloped; we can picture life in a little family like this as a state in which what we call the individual is altogether absent. There is consequently no perception of death in our sense. My reflections on this accident at the breakfast table simultaneously shed light on another question.

When we are able to form a conclusion like this, we may be sure that the same is hidden in our own lives. This is in fact the case here too, though not within the family; for this ancient form of blindness reigns where we would least suspect—in regard to our own I. We do not perceive our own self as individual; an image of our own corpse also eludes our imagination. In our highly complex inner order, the I is the last stronghold into which this life-blindness has retreated; and from there, it ventures forth.

With regard at first to the corpse, this assertion may appear pointless, since, by all accounts, people and objects are cut off from any perception. Yet this is not entirely true. In this regard, something I heard from a young soldier whose arm had been blown off struck me as remarkable. He told me that he had so fully retained awareness that it had occurred to him to loosen his watch on the arm that had just been sliced off by a grenade splinter. But in this attempt, he realized that the arm was no longer at his disposal and that he had not in the least grasped the loss. Death is a further separation, by which we rid ourselves of the totality of our members. This corresponds to what is related in the Tibetan Book of the Dead: according to it, a brief period of unconsciousness follows death; however, shortly thereafter, the departed returns to the place of death, where he first guesses his new condition from the grieving of his relatives.

In the same measure, we are life-blind with respect to our body, and even to our spirit. This touches on the often ghostly aspect of mirror images. The mirror of society develops a picture for us in the same way, which we become accustomed to call our individuality. But, fundamentally, everything that is ours in this sense actually has nothing at all to do with us. By no coincidence, our own era grants new insights here. Kubin[50] recently related to me how he had been filmed during some everyday activities: at breakfast, in the garden, at his worktable. He very effectively described the film's effect on him as the "astonishment that I had mistaken myself for that 60-year-old over there."

Our senses as a whole, and not just our eyes, resemble a mirror, in that they look outwardly and are blind on the back side. Our eyes turn the *tapetum negrum* toward us, so that we live in the blind spot of ourselves. Our faces and movements in film appear to us as those of a

50. Alfred Kubin (1877–1959), an Austrian graphic artist, one of the few contemporary artists whom Jünger truly appreciated. Jünger was particularly influenced by Kubin's only novel, *The Other Side* (1908), a surrealistic depiction of the ultimate dissolution of a decadent world. Kubin also provided sketches for Jünger's account of his travels in Norway, *Myrdun*.

stranger; our recorded voices sound unfamiliar. Even our own photo embarrasses us, and we usually only reluctantly acknowledge it as ours. As a doctor, we cannot cure ourselves, and as an artist or an author we cannot judge our own style. Basically, everyone thinks highly of his or her own performance and is never surprised by applause; likewise, every woman thinks herself pretty. We always see ourselves as identical with blind will, with the formless life-force that fills us—yet our particularities, our way of living, are only known from outside. Even in the case of the gifted, this relation hardly changes; it is thus astounding how frequently even exceptional people prefer their weakest sides. The reason is that they value the part of their art that most engages their will.

And yet, as much as anyone noticing this form of life-blindness cannot deny its existence, nonetheless we are not entirely under its spell. This is already shown by our ability to describe it; and this response represents an important act, for beyond it awaits a clear, deep, and differentiated understanding of life and its orders along lines of spiritual relationship. There an individual may truly achieve that extraordinary level of enlightenment in which he is able to see himself from a distance. Developed law, the state, and great historiography are based on this virtue—as the essential traits of an imperial power that commands peoples, and that are united in a Caesar. This superior man speaks rightly of himself in the third person. And had *this* not entered history, we would live like termites in edifices that are not states but large nests where life-blindness is king.

In this sense, "Know thyself" remains the relevant heraldic motto for us all. For each of us constantly senses the mighty pull of the dark night of life that wants to suck us into it. There exists a tremendous striving, disguised under constantly changing forms, which aims to fully recapture our lives into the law of the brood, into the darkness of the womb. There is no happiness there, no great men, and no law beyond a profound, blind solidarity.

There lie our roots—but of both, of light and darkness, are our lives woven.

Notes on the Redstart — *Leisnig*

From this observation, it becomes clear to me among other things why nature appears to have proceeded so carelessly in the case of the cuckoo. The difference between a young cuckoo growing up with wrens and its nest companions is so extraordinary that the foster parents' equanimity in putting up with the fraud has always been regarded as a miracle of nature. But of course if the occupants of a wren's nest perceive each other not as life images but as living forces, then similarity of appearance is clearly less a concern for the cuckoo than other forms of assimilation.

In researching our synonyms, there is still much to be discovered; and a form of twin research could also be developed in philology. For instance, the word *corpse*[51] is clearly a magical word by which we characterize the dead in a very specific way. It corresponds to the Roman *imago* as the magical life image concealed in the shrine of the body. *Cadaver,*[52] the designation for that which is merely similar to the dead person, has its own special character, namely, the idea that this shell attracts alien powers, like an abandoned vessel. The dead are thus specially safeguarded and monitored right up to the burial. A singular occupational expression can be noticed on the faces of the personnel working here.

Incidentally, the vocal *ei* often serves to sound things that are a bit spooky. I heard this in an almost pure form, albeit with a little Saxon, in a word used here for such ill-famed places as the gallows hill on the far side of the hollow. It is said to be *eerie*[53] there.

Regarding mirror images let me briefly also mention an unusual phenomenon that will immediately ring a bell with those who have encountered it. If we happen to observe an accident on the street or from a house window, we will be momentarily dazed or stunned. If we also happen to be near a mirror at that moment, we will notice that an awareness of the identity between our mirror image and ourselves has disappeared. A stranger stares at us from out of the glass. This shows that we have sunk deep into the stream of destiny. It is also one reason why mirrors are cloaked in houses where a death has occurred.

Balearic Walks — *Puerto Pollensa, Illa d'Or*

After bathing, I rested in a cork-oak forest in which grazing sheep had been gnawing on the blooming myrtle. Their scent still hung in the bright

51. The German word *Leichnam* in the original is compounded from the Old High German *lih* (body) and *hamo* (cloth).

52. *Leiche* in the original.

53. The original is *eiersch*. "Weird" might be another fitting translation, particularly regarding the vocal *ei*.

air between the thorny underbrush and I soon noticed about thirty pairs of scarab beetles clearing away the droppings. They did not belong to any of the species I know from Sicily, but rather to the wide-necked form of the western Mediterranean, which is distinguished by deeply striped, jet-black wing cases. Their activity evoked a highly intelligent, almost human impression, particularly when they deployed themselves like little workmen to deal with the large balls. Like Gulliver, I hunched deep down over their work, because their convivial hustle and bustle gave a very strong illusion that speech must have been happening down there. But in the still warm morning, I could only hear the quiet scraping of the armored limbs and the dry whirring of the approaching and departing insects, which brought to mind the sound of a tiny airfield. For the first time, I also comprehended the wonderful form of the flying animal as depicted in Egyptian reliefs.

In the afternoon, I located a solitary island of rock, whose steep ridge covered with honey-colored wood spurge rose up out of the fields. I heard sounds everywhere in the scorched bushes—not the evenly drawn-out winding of snakes, but rather the short, rummaging rustle of lizards. The Balearic Islands have conserved some exquisite varieties of them. After I had waited a little on a rock, they came out, often so close that they almost scurried over my feet. I was particularly amused by one that suddenly materialized on a tree root and let its tail hang down like a bridal train. As it raised its head a little to the sun, its throat flashed in the light like blue lapis.

Encounters like these have a startling effect on us—a sort of giddiness elicited by the immediate proximity of the depths of life. The animals usually also enter our perception as quiet and unnoticed as magical images. Through their figures, dances, and games, they then present us with visions of a highly confidential and compelling kind. It seems that every animal image corresponds to a signal in our innermost depths; since I no longer enjoy hunting, I perceive this all the more keenly. All the same, the connections operating here are of a highly cryptic character—we intuit them as we divine the significant content of a sealed letter.

On my return journey, a glorious quartet of color was revealed to me: a fiery geranium shrub growing in front of a blue and white wall, in such a way that the green foliage lay over the blue lower half of the wall, the red crown of blossoms over the white upper half. The houses reposed peacefully in the still air, each wrapped in a delicate veil of smoke. A wanderer here dips into their spheres as if penetrating rings of incense—their hearths are fed with the fragrant wood of mountain pines.

The pleasure afforded by these lonesome passages is certainly also due to the fact that the wanderer, like Bias,[54] "takes everything he owns with himself." His awareness accompanies him like a spherical mirror, or better, like an aura whose center he is. Lovely images penetrate this aura and undergo an atmospheric transformation. In this manner, he proceeds beneath signs like under northern lights, sun halos, and rainbows.

This exquisite marriage and creative union with the world is one of the highest pleasures given us. The earth is our eternal mother and mistress, and like every woman, she rewards us according to our own riches.

The Hippopotamus ***Goslar***

I had been summoned to Preston to consult in a case of incapacitation.

I understood right away that it was one of those instances where our expertise fails, where the diagnosis already comprehends the prognosis as an irrevocable decree—here the appearance of a disorientation not infrequent in patients in their middle years, which announces itself in a speech disorder. This is a fatal portent.

Under these circumstances, my job did not take long, and since the post train would only leave at noon the next day, I found myself banished for a whole day to this unfamiliar city. Yet occasions like this suit me just fine, since my spirit never enjoys a greater freedom of movement than in the mazes of these harbor cities, where foreign folk circle about me like bustling ants. This kind of enlightened disposition arises with particular strength when the local language is unintelligible to me; when I was in India with Wellesley, I often passed weeks with such an illuminated outlook. The magic here might be based on our greater dependence on our eyes in these moments, so that life becomes more distinct in its nature as drama. The whole human social to-do then appears to us as if on stage, at once simplified and deepened. Its images possess a radiant transparency, and its everyday activities gain spiritual power, as though they no longer concerned trade and commerce but

54. *Sapiens omnia sua secum portat*: "A wise man takes everything he owns with himself." Attributed by Cicero to Bias of Priene, a Greek philosopher and one of the Seven Sages of Greece.

instead performances of magic. The world becomes lighter and more transparent, and at the same time we move more boldly and freely in it, like invisible beings. In the hustle and bustle of oriental bazaars, people and things thus often appear to me as though illuminated by glittering torches and shone through with bright, glowing red.

Immersed in such recollections, I roamed aimlessly through the streets and squares until a fog rose up from the sea. When we have once lived life to the fullest, we are thereafter immune to eccentricity and boredom; the memories protect us like a talisman from the ambushes of time. And so the time flew by as in a dream, until the hour the street-lights were lit; and since I love recording such days with a keepsake, I turned off into the antique dealers' lane. Here one finds furniture, works of art, and fine porcelain, but also cheap curiosity shops in which bizarre objects gather dust, like those brought back from voyages by sailors: dried-out porcupine fish, exotic weapons, and the always-present ships in bottles.

So I was all the more amazed when I noticed, instead of these typical shelf-warmers, a lovely watercolor in one of the small display windows; it was framed in brown mahogany and had a signature on its broad, somewhat yellowed margin. Floating on the crisply painted clouds, I deciphered a dedication of the artist to Lord Barrymore[55]—from the date, I presume it referred to the Barrymore who had brought himself to rapid ruin as the orgiastic companion of the Prince Regent. The picture portrayed a Pomeranian tenant farm, a modest enterprise lying in the middle of rich, green meadowlands. The house was depicted in profile; on the living side of the building, the smooth, thatched gables slanted

55. Lord Barrymore, an eighteenth-century English nobleman, known for his great inherited wealth, his love of boxing, cock-fighting, and coach-driving, his foul-mouth when angry, and his friendship with the Prince Regent, George IV. Included in this last was his participation at the debaucheries of Carlton House, where he was a constant visitor. Carlton House, the Prince Regent's residence, was described by Robert Huish in *Memoirs of George IV* as a sort of "royal brothel," where "bacchanalian orgies . . . of a most extraordinary description" took place, a place resembling "more the interior of a Turkish seraglio, than the abode of a British Prince."

On the other hand, like the Prince Regent, Barrymore was reputedly also a man of the arts, of literary and musical talent, and a patron of drama. When the Prince Regent discarded his favorite, Barrymore left Carlton House, ruined in health and reputation, and was plagued to his death by gout and other diseases. On his deathbed, he was apparently haunted by what he might have become and what he had in fact been.

almost down to the ground, while on the other the roof was pitched like the worn-out awning of a tent. There the gables partly abutted a shed filled with hay, from which a hippopotamus fed, as though from a fodder rack. The arrangement of the small farmstead with the oversized animal would certainly have befuddled the eye, were the meadows not so extensive that the row of ancient oaks framing them was foreshortened to minuscule dimensions. Pictorially, this green area provided a counterbalance to the slate-gray mass of the animal, and logically too it appeared normal to find this great glutton in the midst of these lush pastures.

Since capriccios like this have always given me more pleasure than the usual horse races and foxhunts, I went in. The business seemed to have been recently founded, because the space was almost full with still unopened crates. On top of one crate, whose construction recalled a human shape, sat the antiquarian, a young man dressed in an untypically refined manner for his profession. My entry interrupted his examination of a copperplate engraving, whose signature he was scrutinizing with a round, silver-framed magnifying glass. In truth, I was not surprised after I had mentioned the watercolor to him that he greeted me by name—it did enjoy an undeniable repute in the kingdom. Neither did his immediate invitation to join him in his private rooms appear to me as anything more than the usual courtesy.

Extraordinary, on the other hand, I immediately found the two liveried hunters, who, once we had walked through some red curtains, I saw standing in an expectant demeanor by the open fireplace. We had entered a sort of antechamber, in which were laid out a ladder and a number of other apparatuses, such as decorators use to fit out homes. A red cord hung down from the ceiling, evidently for a chandelier. The plasterwork also seemed unfinished, since a mortar and trowels lying in a wooden trough were visible through a half-opened cellar door.

It was not so much these unusual aspects of the scene that made the adventure seem suspicious, as it was a definite atmosphere that rarely deceives in such matters. When a personal assault is in the offing, an electric charge forms between the parties, which no one can misconstrue who has been received in the palaces of Asian princes or negotiated between the ceremonial tents of two armies poised for battle, as I have. After my studies, in my dealings with the insane, I had had abundant opportunity to develop this gift, because in this field even the sharpest observation fails if it is not supported by a kind of intuitive ability.

In such situations, I always find it advisable to let the actions follow smoothly one after another and to avoid any pauses, any cracks by which some or other incident could gain entry—because I have often observed that a free and easy artlessness gives us an exorcising power over base things. And so I did not hesitate in following the antiquarian, who opened a second set of curtains and behind them some double doors, and then withdrew with a bow.

The room he had showed me into revealed itself as a salon preserved in the taste of the previous century, illuminated by many candles and mirrors, with a very beautiful Watteau over the high fireplace. I saw a lady in the middle of the room, who, almost as if in a puppet show, gestured to me to approach. In the nearly shadowless light that came from the unwavering candles, I at once recognized her as that prominent woman whose destiny the world took special interest in at that moment and who had already been long surrounded by gossip. Since I had already seen her livery, I thought it appropriate to bow, as is due in royal palaces. The princess thanked me and bid me take a seat across from her at the small table, whose tabletop consisted of an oval mirror painted with colorful flowers.

After we had been sitting a long while silently observing each other, I could not, despite the questionable circumstances of my entrance, resist my fondness for physiognomy, which had developed in me since the period of my work on the facial expressions of the mentally ill and which was often bothersome and a little absurd even to me. This inclination, which I often indulged during my long night walks in Ostend by letting the myriad faces glide by me in a kaleidoscopic manner, had endowed me with a fatally sharp eye that to some extent allowed me to divine the germs of the bizarre in advance. This talent is all the more distressing to me, because, in direct contrast to our times, I perceive in that which is regular and law-conforming the grandeur that keeps man connected to the divine. As a physician, I unfortunately often fare as I did back in the Bengali woodlands, where I watched with dread how the forms of life suffocated from their own excesses. So too it seems to me that a profusion of symptoms actually separates us like an impenetrable thicket from our patients—we know too little about health and too much about sicknesses.

Indeed, in the case at hand, a coarser eye might have seen the incipient disorder. However, as experience shows, it takes a long time before the full extent of the matter becomes clear. This is particularly true where the ruling ideas are logically, even ingeniously interconnected, though all the while under the power of delusion—like a boat that is steered with perfect navigational confidence into the reef. When the patient is moreover in a high position, the censure usually comes only hesitantly, and so the powerful have the advantage over the small folk that they are able to carry on longer in their folly.

Let me also say here that I regard the astrologers' practice of investigating similarities with animals as a good means of physiognomic knowledge. In this context, I found the snake-like very strongly expressed here, indeed so strongly that at its appearance I felt the same interest as in the garden of my pavilion when I encountered the great Naja,[56] which is considered the queen of snakes. This habitus tends to develop in people where prominent cheekbones are united with a certain weakness in the maxillary parts, as is not uncommonly seen in just these old families. Intensifying the impression here in an almost frightening manner was also a swaying movement of the throat and the fixed yet prying glance of the large eyes.

A second facial feature struck me no less strongly, something I characterize in my "Physiognomics" as the scorched. This facial expression is found where the life-light has been intensified to a flame; it can be perceived in lives of vice or misfortune, but most keenly when both are present together. From a face like this, a very definite evolution may be inferred, in particular one filled with mad jealousy or scorned love. Above all, we encounter it in women upon whose lives the oncoming aging already casts its shadows.

If I have portrayed this somewhat discursively, then I would add in my defense that our silence occupied a long span of time—and these remarks capture the mood that animates me in such situations very well. My thoughts follow one another like the individual chimes in a ringing

56. *Naja* is a genus of venomous snakes, including the group commonly known as cobras.

of bells, yet each is enveloped in its own vibrant aura. I must also admit, that through this reading of the face, I almost forgot the strangeness of the circumstances. It has always been part of the Great Hunt for me to look into a person's eyes and then sink my gaze to that ambiguous and amorphous object that stirs on the crater floor. But here this capacity allowed me to guess the matter at hand before a word had been uttered.

At last my counterpart exclaimed with a transparent, studied laugh: "Doctor, you must admit that I understand the bait needed to catch such fish."

"And with pleasure even, your Highness—nothing could have lured me in more surely than that watercolor. And given this fact, may I also assume that my role as consultant here in Preston has a secret history?"

"I see that your shrewdness is admired with reason; they also say that you had exceptional teachers. And that is why I brought about this meeting; I need your professional assistance in an immensely difficult matter."

"My skills are at your disposal. But wouldn't it have been easier to avail yourself of my services at my house in Russell Square rather than in this almost magical manner?"

"Absolutely not, because it would have been extremely questionable for more than one reason if we were seen together. This also concerns matters of such consequence that I hardly dare mention them aloud. Now listen."

The moment she leaned toward my ear, I sensed that the time had come to give the affair the twist that I intended to warrant my safety. I thus took the liberty of placing my hand on the arm of this still-attractive woman, an arm barely covered by a sleeve of pale-red silk gauze that harmonized wonderfully with a marvelous gown of pearl-gray Utrecht velvet.

"Your Highness will excuse the interruption, but the consultation already began when I entered the room. I well expect that you intend to reveal one of those secrets that are reserved for the great of this world, the knowledge of which cannot be kept well enough guarded. Fortunately, insights of this nature are not required for the cure. Moreover, the means at our disposal are such that the patient's story is a source of only secondary importance; and there are cases where we may pronounce absolution without any preceding confession. I would therefore ask your

Highness to restrict herself to those aspects of the affair that are appropriate for the physician—this could also have benefits for the measures to be implemented."

As I said this, I noticed the face of the princess begin to gradually brighten. Incidentally, this is the effect that a physician must initially and primarily bring about, if he is to merit the title of physician; his first power of healing must lie in his voice. These days, as we begin turning our attention to the treatment of the parts, in the healing arts as much as in mechanics, so the elements fade into obscurity, and we cannot reproach the common folk who swear by their snake-oil sellers and witch doctors.

But in regard to this case, it is far from my mind to believe that things still proceed as they did in old Danish castles, because even the time of the Iron Mask is long since over. Meanwhile, we live in an age that gobbles up Scott's historical novels[57] and has an odd sense for theatrical repetition. And casualties can also happen today—anyone falling in a duel now is as dead as he was then, even though the chivalrous lifestyle has long since vanished. But above all else, that thing whose cognizance or, much more, whose utterance I wanted to avoid was already aflame with the light of madness, and under such circumstances there is always danger, particularly when the patient holds the reins of power. I already sensed the almost supernatural manner in which I had been summoned as ominous, and thus I had plenty of reason to hold back. In countries where there exist numerous rooms in both public and private buildings that are only entered at mortal peril, one gains a good education in discretion.

After my patient had listened carefully to me, and as I said, with growing cheerfulness, I watched her walk reflectively a good while up and down the room, with the swaying motion of her head transferred in a gracious manner to her body. At last she tugged on the silken bell cord hanging next to the door. The young antiquarian reappeared and received some instructions from her in a quiet voice, of which I understood no more than the Italian word "presto." A moment later, I heard noises in the antechamber. Then she returned to the mirror table and now placed her hand on my arm.

57. Sir Walter Scott (1771–1832), the Scottish historical novelist, playwright, and poet.

"Sir, under the circumstances, you can make me a more significant service than I had thought. What I have to share with you now is quickly said, though expressing even this little is painfully embarrassing for me. But, since we also expose ourselves physically to our doctors without coverings..."

"Speak without reserve, Madam."

"Well. Since the...since the incident I alluded to, unexpected disorders have materialized, at first only mildly, but then increasingly troubling to me. Lately, I feel like I am in a rapidly sinking ship.... Doctor, I have moments when everything begins to waver, and if anyone can help me, it is you."

"I assume you are also not satisfied with your nightly sleep."

"As a matter of fact, very unsatisfied, but don't think me fastidious. Even at fourteen, I took the liberty of passing delectable night-hours with forbidden readings in the style of Lucian,[58] and not even Duncan's ghost would disturb me. But there exist more malevolent things than these, processes of a quasi-mechanical nature, like an automaton that begins to purr."

"Do you have the impression that those near you are already aware of these crises?"

"No, not really, I could always plead migraines as an excuse. However, during every conversation, at every reception, I feel like I am moving through rooms where the air brims with powder and sparks fly—and this all the more intensely the more distinguished the circles I find myself in. Naturally, the whole affair also has a smack of the ridiculous that permeates life like bad spice, and this in itself often fills me with burning anger. In the beginning, when I thought of that...that incident, it was no more than one memory among all the other kinds of memories, like a particular fish that reappeared now and then on the surface. Perhaps it was due to my efforts to repress this memory in particular that its resurfacing began to disconcert me. I noticed that a kind of soliloquy accompanied these efforts, at first as isolated words, then as sentences, and in the end as explosions of flaming, screaming rage. With it came a mania for using filthy expressions—filthier than anything from the fish markets or before the executions at Newgate. In fact,

58. Presumably referring to Lucian of Samosata (c. AD 125–after 180), a rhetorician and satirist who wrote in Greek. He is noted for his witty and scoffing nature.

I have discovered in myself a talent for coming up with curses unheard of even in the sewers, just as if newly discovered fountains of filth were emptying into me…"

"Please continue, Madam."

"It also seems to me that these masses are bottling up in me, as it happens before a mill weir. And so I take advantage of every opportunity to shed some of this burden through secretly discharged maledictions, or to write them down in letters that I then burn. But after days of ceremonials where I am constantly under the public eye from morning to night, I feel a kind of lava rising up in me. And so recently, on the eve of the first of May, it came to an appalling outburst, during which I was like a stranger to myself. Around midnight, I caught a glimpse of myself floating in the large mirror of my dressing room, candle in hand, foaming at the mouth and with frighteningly bristling hair. Since then, I seem to have been endowed with an especially penetrating glance, so that I perceive all that is base in the faces and in the voices, and every obliging word, every courtly gesture appears to me as an all-too-perfunctorily, all-too-airily staged deceit that covers up some secret conniving. The more magnificent the gleam of the pomp and uniforms, the more the discrepancy becomes apparent. When the envoys present their important foreign visitors or when I am sitting at a magnificent banquet table, I am overcome by the desire to tear off my clothes and make a toast that would expose the very entrails of the earth. But Doctor, this is not what upsets me, because even as a child, whenever I had an exquisite glass in my hand, I felt the urge to hurl it onto the stone floor, and I never climbed a cliff or a tower without a hidden voice daring me to jump. But there is something beyond this, an unknown, which plays with me like a cat with a mouse. It is not what I think that horrifies me; instead, I want to ask you this: what am I supposed to do if it comes over me again like on that night?"

After I had heard this report, which was even a little more comprehensive, we slipped back into silence. For a long while I contemplated the exquisite pearls that lay scattered across the carpet—because in mentioning her fit, the princess had grabbed her necklace and the strand had broken under her hand. Before a single pearl of the size of hers here is found in the Maldives or Bahrain, two pearl slaves have wasted away from emaciation and a third has been speared by a swordfish.

It was certainly not the question she directed to me that now occupied my thoughts. Very different things usually concern the patient and the physician—when I cured my friend Wallmoden of his abscess, he was mostly worried about his complexion, which he found a little yellowish. Something I have often observed seems so characteristic of people: that a spiritual threat usually only becomes apparent to them when they also sense their will impinged on. For a physician, it makes little difference whether the patient conceals the delusion within him or whether he thinks himself driven from without. In both cases, the cure happens at the roots. Of course theoretically, that extraordinary moment when our will appears to abandon us remains highly significant, because our intellectual powers, like our muscles, have their own voluntary and involuntary apparatuses, and anyone who understands the rules that govern the interplay of these two, like the phases of the sun and the moon, has achieved a level in this art that we could not even dream about. I myself have learned more from my intimate associations with men who have mastered their breath and pulse and whose skin is invulnerable to fire than in I did in Hunter's anatomical theater—and even there I learned plenty. Here is the basis of the spontaneous cures of falling sickness and other maladies that have established my reputation; their simple secret lies in passing sovereignty over certain parts of my patients' vegetative system into their own hands.

Consequently, it should be evident that I could not be taken aback by phenomena I had often enough seen vanish like smoke under the manipulations of dervishes, yellow-robed monks, or sharply pungent Capuchins. Such cures intersect with the practices of goateed priesthoods, whose mysteries have always created meaning for the simple folk and their women. But in addition to understanding the type and origin of the disorder here, I am also not inexperienced in treating it—and because in some sense this very disorder is an aspect of our inventory of national maladies, its motif resurfaces in me during each of the evening walks I take from the palaces on the west side over to those quarters where misery circles greedily around its dark antipode of power. This is a double-dealing that recurs in our literature as well, wherein the spirit is reflected as though in a silver mirror and in a black one. It is also not surprising that we hear it sound where the individuals sink into confusion; initiates are also acquainted with the secret festivities that recall the

Lupercalia of the Roman Faunus, in whose circles our society debauches itself. Though far from sanctioning these spectacles that find their woeful epitome in Carlton House, I nevertheless have them to thank for certain insights, since the elevated and the base also play into each other here in a remarkable way. It often seems to me that such excesses reflect the negative side of a virtue, and by this I refer to the inner distance that legitimizes our dominion over a populace. Late at night on the old London Bridge, when I contemplate the dark waters with the tall arches of gray stone planted in them, I feel a waft of pride and grandeur grazing my temples. Then a shudder comes over me and I eagerly throw a copper coin down into its glimmering, nocturnal depths.

But I do not want to digress. The affliction often projects like a stigma into the sphere of the body, and it is not a physician who is then called for. However I had recognized the situation I found myself in, and I could deliver what was expected of me. I therefore gave my instructions.

"It honors me, Your Highness, that I may serve you. First and foremost, I advise you to make a quick transfer to Cheltenham; the timing is good, as the bathing season there has not yet begun. You will pass your days there keeping to a diet, both alone and in company. You must repulse the urge to soliloquies, though without exertion. When the inner compulsion becomes too powerful, articulate the mantra I am writing down for you here in a moderate voice. Should you be in company, I would ask you to recite it mentally while touching your necklace with your hand. For the time being, you can substitute your pearls with water chestnuts. But I very much doubt that this state will arise if Your Highness partakes of the fondant that I am prescribing for you to take to receptions. It will, as it were, rein in the tongue; I'm also going to mix in a drug that will deepen your nightly sleep. I also particularly recommend the use of incense sticks, which should be burned at night on an earthen plate and added generously to the open fire during the day. I will leave everything necessary for you enciphered in my small dispensary, which Mister Morrison operates in his pharmacy. I'll include a point book, like those used by spiritual orders for examinations of conscience, which I always provide as a spiritual mirror to my patients that live far away. Follow my advice and I can promise that the disturbances will abate within a month. Finally, I would also consider it beneficial if Your Highness enlisted one of our little country priests as a secretary. You will find excellent characters there, certainly a match for any antiquarians."

After I had explained my prescription in detail, the princess, rising, granted me permission to withdraw. It almost seemed to me that she had guessed more than I intended, because she surprised me by reciprocating with that antiquated courtly bow in which a knee and a hand brush the ground. Perhaps it was only a gesture that her pride demanded of her. As she made this compliment, she picked up the solitaire pearl of the necklace, an immaculate sphere the size of a marble cherry with a marvelous play of colors. In this manner, an ornament of beauty came my way the likes of which even Lord Clive[59] had never nabbed.

As the antiquarian led me out, I noticed that the antechamber had already been cleared out. The fire was extinguished, the cellar doors closed, the ladder and the chandelier cord gone, and even the hunters were no longer leaning on the fireplace. The room was as empty as a stage at a cancelled performance. It is not my encounters with the peculiar that keep surprising me in my profession. It seems far more unusual to me that every mania finds as many helpers as it needs. And since our world nonetheless follows its path so unswervingly, I cannot question that all is ordered according to a wise plan.

It is not only the majestic pearl that reminds me of the mists of Preston when I contemplate it at night under good candlelight. About six weeks later, a large, flat crate was delivered to my house in the city, and packed carefully inside I found the watercolor of the Pomeranian tenant farm. I hung it on a strong red cord over the fireplace, not directly over my workplace but also not too far away from it. Once in a while, I notice when one of my guests intently examines it and at last turns away, as if it were an optical illusion. This includes my friend Wallmoden, who has admittedly become somewhat fastidious since his abscess. As a result, I will not argue with him that the picture belongs among the bizarre artworks. In this way, I can keep it to myself that the dissonances of our beautiful world have often lured me like barred portals up to the

59. Major-General Robert Clive (1725–1774), known as Clive of India, a British officer who established the military and political supremacy of the East India Company in Bengal. He is credited with securing India, and the wealth that followed, for the British crown. After the battle of Plassey in Bengal, the newly installed Nawab allowed him to take all the gold and jewels he wanted from the defeated Nawab's treasury, and he became vastly wealthy as a result.

higher echelons of their harmony—and that I find the danger a small toll to pay.

The Apricot ***Geneva***

Shortly after Lausanne, my eyelids closed in the moving train. The story of a marriage I dreamed about was first heard in words. But then—it concerned the start of a quarrel—the circumstances manifested visibly, as a colorful fruit that appeared before my eyes and began to revolve slowly on its stem. Its colors played from ripe yellow to a violet speckled with darker spots. The further course of things became apparent, without need of a single word, through the degree of discoloration, the number of spots, and their relative positions. In this manner, the proceedings could be seen in the highest clarity, not only in all their details, but also in their secret meaning, the way a melody is read from a sheet of music.

Remarkably, the scene, though actually a sad one, cheered me up; this must be because it represented a human relationship from its necessary or—as a painter would understand it—its pictorial aspect. I had the impression that this all took no longer than the batting of the eyelids.

First Postscript ***Casablanca***

We can generally add here how favorable a sudden awakening is for the recollection of dream images. A nice analogy presented itself today near Ain Diab, whose barren lands I hiked through at midday hunting for cave animals. Its cracked red earth, on which white Narcissi bloomed now at the end of December, was strewn with large rocks. Since these blocks are of calcareous tuff, they are easily turned over. With a little luck, one finds a great blue Carabus under them, an insect found only in the territory around Casablanca, or assorted other creatures escaping the scorching rays of the sun. Among many other animals, I caught glimpses of a sand-colored gecko, a very slender colorful snake rolled up like a whiplash, and a great Mauritanian scorpion.

All this depends greatly on flipping the rock over with a quick movement. The company gathered beneath holds its position a short while, frozen by the sudden incidence of the light, so that the eye is able to capture them. If the block is turned over slowly, they find time to slip away through a hundred fissures and holes and a final blurred scurrying is all we glimpse.

In just this manner, a sudden awakening resembles a quickly drawn aside curtain. We then realize the unusual company we keep at night. A particular manner of seeing is involved here, of which we are capable for only a brief moment—perhaps not longer than the time we sit half-upright in the dark, after being jolted awake. The figures then dissipate—and everyone knows the strained effort with which we try to recall this or that detail.

In exceptional cases, it may be possible that a person can extend or exploit this form of insight at will. This gift is revealed in the pictures of Hieronymus Bosch. We get the impression that the carousing rabble on which we eavesdrop would instantly vaporize if it realized that a human eye was regarding it. We spy on the scene as if through the closed canopy of a ceiling.

There are also extraordinary states in which we linger up in this ceiling, though already awake. This happens above all when the awakening is at once sudden and frightful. Our eyes flash open, and we see the house in flames. We jump up and walk in a waking dream through the burning corridors and steps down to the entrance. We move as if gliding, without a sense of gravity, while terror and a sort of delight accompany us.

This is one of the rare states in which a man acts like a ghost. I like to imagine Medea[60] in this kind of terrible exaltation. The waking and dreaming states are inverted here, as are our power and expression of feeling, like the plus and minus signs of a higher mathematics; in the same way, laughing and weeping are interchanged in a horrible manner.

Time and again, tragedies are written whose authors live in apparent ignorance of the tragic elements. The characters then resemble those drawn by the blind with a stencil.

Second Postscript ***Überlingen***

Over the years, dream lore has been assigned to the most varied disciplines, including soothsaying, symbolism, medicine, and, most recently, psychology. An attempt to relate dreams to physics may still seem a

60. In Euripedes' play *Medea*, based on the myth of Jason and Medea, Medea, the barbarian wife of Jason, revenges his abandoning of her in order to marry Glauce, daughter of King Creon, by poisoning Creon and Glauce. In a passionate fit of revenge, she then also stabs her own sons to death.

remote curiosity to the mind. Yet the spoils it would gather there would surprise and even shock it.

The dream world appears to be enclosed in an impervious capsule or *camera obscura*, within which the images are subject to special rules. The entry of daylight or consciousness at first induces paralysis, then a deterioration of the figures. The relations there between the light and dark realms resemble those of photography. We thus find that a sudden incidence of consciousness is more conducive to the recollection of dream images than a gradual awakening. If we are awakened at night by a dream and then reflect on it, it also returns more easily in the morning.

These kinds of memories have no resemblance at all to those connected with our waking state. They are characterized by a remarkable fragility. Daylight leeches away their color, so that after an hour they have become as pale as an unwritten page or badly fixed film. Then again, a dream that we believe to have registered in our consciousness in the morning like any other thing may already be forgotten by midday. The colors here are of a particularly ephemeral nature, and the characters are painted in invisible inks that disappear or reappear in an incomprehensible manner.

The following is also revealing: it is not uncommon for an isolated dream fragment to float by us during the day like the fringe of a dress, which our mind immediately tries to grasp. But as we reflect on them, these perceptions disappear like smoke, and all the more rapidly the more we strain ourselves. During a period in which I sometimes made notes on dreams in the middle of the night, I would try to walk from the bedroom to the library with closed eyes.

Certain dream fragments stick in our memory like rocks from alien planets embedded in the earth's crust. Unusual fruits may be harvested here, such as the remarkable light that illuminates the dream world. Perhaps an unlimited diffraction is what distinguishes it, or maybe it is coated onto the forms like a phosphoric substance. In any case, we do not perceive shadows in dreams, only differing shades of darkness. Colors are also usually absent, or we see a spectrum of tones like that in caves or on moonlit nights.

Perception in general takes place under different conditions here. The spirit operates almost entirely without concepts and instead with instruments of a superior sensuousness. There is also no clear separation between the spirit and the representational world, and as a result, the spirit enters this world with lightning speed and is not limited to its surfaces. It does not perceive this world as the eye perceives things in the light, but rather penetrates it totally, as a radiant ether with special powers. Hence, when we converse or argue with someone in a dream, we know exactly what they feel and think; our perception sees through them without resistance or settles at will within them. Likewise, we seldom use the door in a dream; we pass through the walls and ceilings. We resemble electrical current, which flows now through human bodies, now animals, now even inanimate things, right into their atoms. Our power of vision is also not limited to our eyes—the dream world is like a plant onto whose form we are able to graft our perception at whichever point we like.

The following prospects may also be suggested here, with caution naturally. It may transpire, as with any spiritual exercise, that a mirror image of our attempt to comprehend dreams with exact means presents itself. Roughly speaking, this would appear as foreign elements on their part penetrating the measurable world. In this sense, our physicists' efforts challenge us to a special form of attention. Bold spirits live here—bolder yet than those who ventured out onto the open oceans, they penetrate into profoundly concealed spaces. And in correspondence with these solitary efforts, an echo sounds back from the unknown, like a knocking from the depths of the mine. We sense how the intelligence that animates the substance begins to grow, and we divine the exquisite depths of matter like a new dimension.

Visible processes then correspond to this. For example, it seems that in various domains man is degenerating to a vegetative form of life, which does not contradict technology but is rather orchestrated by it. Above all, we should mention the broad infiltration of rhythmic activity, as well as the changes brought about by high velocity. In broad domains, we increasingly proceed through oscillation and reflex; this is especially true for traffic. This may lead to a reduction of the pain that fills our working world, which is essentially the pain of consciousness. Doors to *désinvolture* may also open at these points—in his little story about the puppet theater, Kleist has already consummately represented how this may be possible. Like the texts of Hoffmann and E. A. Poe, this story contains an as-yet-undiscovered preview on our mechanical world. Ultimately, I think the claims that our cinema and radio shows are more closely related to the world of dream images than to our traditional theatre will also be corroborated.

In this state, in which new powers enter under extraordinary disguises—because it is always consciousness itself that spins the magic hoods and cloaks for them—in this state, a heightened responsibility falls to the spirit, as it does at every twilight. It cannot limit itself to the controls that its sciences offer. For the spirit in a special sense, wakefulness and courage are the order of the day.

Third Postscript — ***Überlingen***

This may be the place to touch again on those upper strata mentioned in the "Gravel Pit." In retrospect, it seems to me that this form of model collecting is the one best suited to the enterprise. Only its stenographic character can cope with the richness of the outcroppings—I use this word in its geological sense. At the same time, a prose of higher penetrative power must match the presentation of models. The spirit of language does not lie in the words and images; it is embedded in the atoms, which an unknown current animates and compels into magnetic figures. Only thus is the spirit of language able to grasp the unity of the world, beyond day and night, beyond dream and reality, time and place, friend and foe—under all conditions of spirit and matter.

The Surplus — ***Überlingen***

I first heard Hesiod's saying that mankind's sustenance is concealed from him by the gods so early in life that it sunk in before verifying itself through experience. In the meantime, I have come across increasingly convincing evidence of its validity—often just where abundance seems to reign.

Man's tendency to let part of the fruit of an overabundant harvest rot, rather than lower its price, may belong here. The grounds for this behavior lie deeper than where we seek them today; they apparently involve an innate blindness of the whole species. This can be observed well where an economic system has been changed, so that equal quantities of goods are wasted no longer individually but as part of a planned economy, for instance through misguided distribution. Even during the relatively insignificant improvements we call economic upturns, the unpleasant effects predominate. So, too, a windfall of enormous wealth, the kind most people dream of, rarely turns out for the best. The base ecstasy awakened by the sight of new veins of gold has often been portrayed—a frenzy, closely followed by murder, violence, and finally a senseless dissipation of the treasure. Mankind must search for his food and scrape it out with his own fingers; if it happens to be showered on him, he falls into confusion.

The beggarliness we are driven to in our efforts to develop is also apparent in the sciences. Here we resemble not so much the blind as we do deaf-mutes, whom an unknown and slightly facetious host has invited to the opera. We observe a series of remarkable proceedings on stage and eventually discover a certain correspondence with movements we perceive in the orchestra. A great abundance of shrewd and useful endeavors follows. But it remains eternally concealed from us that everything we circumscribe and classify in this way—the elements, the atoms, life, and light—has its own voice. Indeed, if we could hear this voice, we would be able to fly without planes and our bodies would become transparent to our sight even without X-rays.

Yet our occasionally extravagant imagination gets the better of us, so that we think we can milk the universe with our machines. Even Schopenhauer hoped that these efforts would bring leisure to men and thereby increase their opportunity for contemplation. On the contrary, it is evident that the sudden gain of new powers and methods, which the natural sciences prepare and technology realizes, leads like a whirlwind to an initial bemusement, then to fruitless dissipation. We thus get the impression, as an example, that the army of people providing us with boots and shoes has not shrunk in the last century but grown. And without doubt, more work is in fact performed there now than in the old guilds of Jakob Böhme's or Hans Sachs's times; because it contradicts the sense of mechanics that it augment leisure. On the contrary, it not only captures manpower more keenly, it also rations out sustenance to the individuals more frugally.

And so in every well-thought-out enterprise, like a large hotel for example, a kind of hunger can be sensed, which persists even when everything is present in abundance. When a state sees itself obliged to ration sustenance, this kind of famine with full granaries can spread like panic—full satisfaction requires the perception that there is more on the plate than can be eaten. Therein lies the soothing effect of the still life and of all food displayed in showcases, such as fruits and desserts. In one of the typical storehouses found on every Norwegian farm, a farmer commented as he saw me observing the barrels of flour, bread, ham, sausages, and dried fish: "Maat for et aar," which means, "Food for a year."

Among the great masses inhabiting our cities, not even the richest can claim this. Without distinction, they are all separated from want by the narrowest margin, and in observing them, we may be overcome by a feeling of world-angst, as at the sight of Chinese rivers gushing through towering dams out over the cultivated ground.

Hesiod is correct when he says that a meager harvest has been allotted us, even in a world full of lavish gifts, in which one day's work in a year should more than suffice for all the rest. In seeking to transform wood into bread and atoms into power, our own sciences think the same way. There is nothing utopic in this or in even bolder intentions; but it becomes utopic if we believe that want can be banished in this way. Where such designs do succeed, unanticipated counterbalances reestablish the original equilibrium—for example, the number of mouths to feed increases with the amount of food, or the acquisition of new powers escalates warfare. In this world, Mars has the most insatiable appetite of all.

Certainly, Hesiod's saying, like the moon, only ever shows us its familiar side. But its assumption is that a surplus does exist and that executive power over it lies in the hands of the gods. For life contains two orientations: one directed at needs, the other at the surplus piled around the sacrificial fire. Our sciences are disposed to the need side and are turned away from the feast side; they are intrinsically bound to want, as the measurer is with the measure, the counter with the count. In fact, had it not always existed, science itself should have been forged from this surplus—because it is actually nothing other than theology.

At this point, we find ourselves in a peculiar position and can speak only cautiously. We perceive our world like an iceberg, whose tip alone shows above the surface. Our formulas are undoubtedly becoming more succinct, crystalline, and conclusive, and the day when science has said the final word can already be anticipated. And yet science will never arrive at the highest potential of its constituent elements, that is to say, at the surplus. Here theology is to join in, a new theology possessing descriptive character. Its task is to bestow names on the images long familiar to us. This naming will be accompanied by mighty acts of cognition, of recognition, and of happiness.

In the Shops (2) ***Goslar***

Even in daily life, a fine sense of symbolic relationship attends us and we often take off on remarkable detours seeking out in distant peoples and forgotten times arrangements that surround us seamlessly on all sides. It takes a long time before we realize that we have been superbly equipped with our two eyes and that the nearest street corner suffices to observe all these curious things.

For instance, a man immediately senses the quiet approach of the inappropriate when he enters certain shops such as greengrocers, or indeed has contact with any domain that women rule over. These market shops are found in abundance in the old alleys here, and it is nearly always women who sell there. Upon entering, a man immediately has the feeling of coming across as an alien, and he usually also disturbs a group of women absorbed in confidential matters. *Fama*, the female equivalent of newspapers and politics, is born in such places. It can be sensed right away that matters are managed here in a much finer, apposite, and cryptic manner than in political discussions. Above all, it is the slogans that are missing; remarks are never directed at general concepts but entirely at the person and the specific detail. We occasionally catch a glimpse of the grocer woman's husband, who often exhibits gnome-like traits and is kept busy with menial jobs. He can be seen hauling heavy sacks into the loft and is assigned that part of the business that is performed off-premises, such as bringing in the goods on a small carriage. The shop itself is often down in the cellar, with few windows and usually only a small display window, and the articles are hastily spread out, like on a battlefield altar. The strong earthy smell emanating from cereals predominates. The scale plays a conspicuously minor role here—fruits are far more commonly sold by the piece, bunch, bundle, or container. There is also a clear distaste for the decimal system; the old measures are still used: the dozen, the shock, the score. The measuring containers carry markings whose meanings are barely still known. Wooden devices prevail over iron ones, and knives are rarely used.

What a difference when one enters a butcher shop. Here the light streams through large, ample windows and reflects off scoured tiles and shiny metallic utensils. All is bright and gleaming and filled by a jovial cheerfulness whose masculine origin is unmistakable. The subordinate role falls here to the woman; she serves, takes the money, and has at most a little knife to cut the strings of sausages. The space is commanded by the figure of the master, standing in a blood-spattered apron behind his cutting block, cutting up the large hunks he butchered in the early morning with fellow butchers and apprentices in the slaughterhouse. An almost aggressive attitude prevails with respect to the patrons: weights are rounded up without waiting long for the customer's consent, and heavy bones are tossed in with the meat. One usually also sees excellent decimal scales here. If the master of such an establishment dies, the wife is forced to sell the shop or bring in other journeymen. Such spaces are ruled by a low-grade Mars, whose character is often visible in the faces; its female counterpart is a Venus-type of sanguine fleshiness. The manner in which the utensils resemble weapons of war and yet differ from them is also remarkable—in contrast to battle-axes and swords, the cleavers have wide cutting edges and the knives long handles. A tool that frequently crops up in this and similar contexts is the hook.

Shops in which women are only rarely seen are all those where hardware is sold. Here we most commonly meet farmers and tradesmen, who subject each article to a protracted examination before buying. The numerous articles are stored on well-organized shelves. They have curious names, yet the shopkeeper knows how to find them quickly, like words in a dictionary. The language of smiths is heard here; it suffices for labeling our whole new arsenal of machine technology. It may seem odd to us to learn of peoples in which the smith caste possessed its own language; yet we often see customers entering these shops, whom the salesperson must practically interrogate before he guesses the names of the desired tools or appliances. The customer may even discover that he is planning a procedure for which he does not even know the name.

Buyers leave a hardware shop feeling that they have acquired a good and useful object. In leaving a fabric shop, on the other hand, we immediately wonder if we have been cheated. By their very nature, textiles favor deception; not for nothing do we speak of a tissue, a web, or a mesh of lies. Woven goods must therefore be sold by persuasion;

nowhere else is the same loquacity encountered as where the parties haggle over cloth. This difference carries over to the big picture; it can be sensed in the atmosphere of a whole city whether smiths or weavers reign there. In cities of smiths, things proceed more forcefully, yet freedom is better understood. At the same time, the names of weaver cities have become synonymous with particular forms of exploitation—people can be bound better with threads than with chains.

The Color Blue ***Überlingen***

We are like the little thrushes that Mother Earth entices with the color red. Red is the color of her inner matter, which she conceals under her green dress, her white lace woven of glacial ice and the gray flounces with which the oceans skirt her coasts. We love it when our Mother reveals some of her red secrets to us, we love the splendor of Fafnir's grotto, the blood on hot days of battle, and the full lips that offer themselves, half-opened, to us.

Red is the material of our earthly life, in which we are robed from head to toe. Red is thus close to us—so close that no room for reflection exists between it and us. It is the color of the pure present; in its domain, we come to a wordless accord.

At the same time—to our salvation—powerful seals are placed on this color. We embrace it, and we shrink back as vigorously from it; it makes the breath of life faster, but at the same time more tremulous. Were it otherwise, the world would present a picture like a Bluebeard's chamber, a stage illuminated by the haphazard, pervasive glow of perpetual fires. We are shielded from this fate by the protecting and directing powers—by royal crimson and the pure flame of the vestal hearth.

Though we ascribe this thrift to ourselves, it in fact presupposes the principle of the elevated law-giving spirit to which the color blue is assigned. In this color, both wings of the spirit are denoted: the Miraculous and the Void. It mirrors the mysterious depths and the infinite distances.

Blue is thus above all familiar to us as the color of the sky. Paler and cooler in our latitudes, often verging on gray or green, it evokes empty, boundless space. Only in approaching the tropics does the eternally cheerful Atlantic blue emanate that we can rightly describe as a canopy. But above the earth's haze, the heavenly vault shines in its deepest, nearly black luster, and it may be that the almighty power of the Void reveals itself to the eye here. In the Void, the stars float like crystals in the mother liquor.

The ocean's depths trap blue within them and reflect it varicolored back, from dull cobalt through to bright azure. There are also ocean expanses of silky-dark or sapphire sheen, as well as zones of crystalline lucidity lying over bright sea floors or by rocky whirlpools in which the tide wells up from the depths with the colors of flower calyxes and irises and is marvelously diffused. All lovers of the sea can remember the surprise, followed by bright spiritual cheerfulness, that such spectacles can evoke. It is not the water itself nor its endlessness that brings forth this cheerfulness but rather its divine, neptunian[61] energy, which inhabits even the smallest wave.

Blue is the color of the most distant places and most extreme degrees, cut off from life, like the haze disappearing into the void, like glacial ice, like the heart of a pin-flame. Blue likewise infuses the shadows, the twilight, and the distant plane of the horizon. It draws near to the resting and retreats from the moving.

When the color red appears, we sense an approach and a quickening of relationships—blue on the contrary evokes a feeling of remoteness and hesitation. A garden with blue flowers is thus the most favorable for observation. A room with blue walls will seem larger and quieter, but also colder. For the heart, blue possesses therapeutic power. In popular language, it indicates uncommon, insubstantial, or inebriated states, in particular as the color of air and as a symbol of the magical and of the faithfully steadfast. Indeed, in contrast to polarizing red, blue appears as the natural color of alliances, as the universal color per se. Likewise, it suggests the spiritual and, especially in its violet shades, the carnally unfruitful life.

Blue alludes to the spiritual state, but not to nobility, which is spread across the red tones that predominate in purple. Blue does not participate in differentiation—its home may be supposed where the Law is

61. A probable allusion to Abraham Gottlob Werner's late-eighteenth-century scientific theory of "Neptunism," which explained the formation of rocks by crystallization of minerals in the earth's early oceans. James Hutton's rival theory of "Plutonism" gave a volcanic origin for rock formation. Goethe, who sided with the Neptunists, included a dialogue between a Neptunist and a Plutonist (Mephistopheles) in his *Faust*.

native, not where it reigns. The relations of blue and red offer material for higher meditation: at the cosmic level, on Heaven and Earth, in the human realm, on priestly and royal power.

The Coalfish — ***Bergen***

In the middle of the night, our ship docked in the harbor and the cranes immediately began unloading. Half asleep in my little cabin, I could hear the loads being lifted high up out of the freight holds and then placed on the dockside. This twofold racket, which interrupted a quiet moment, cast me into a bad dream. I felt my clothes caught by one of the hooks and myself hauled up to an immeasurable height, while a crowd of people watched in terror from below. Each time my clothes tore, the hook caught me again by another piece of clothing. With each of these movements, the spectators below cried out loud. But eventually the crane placed me very gently on the ground. People rushed over; I noticed that they were only people I had been disagreeable to and who had tried to harm me in life. It appeared all the more amazing that they looked at me with friendly, moved gazes. They touched and felt me all over with their fingers.

Upon awaking, I went ashore and wandered around Torvet. These Nordic harbor towns remind me of early periods of my childhood; they bore me, but I feel at home in them. Right at that moment, fishing boats that had been out at sea overnight were sailing back into the harbor, and the fish sellers' stands filled with the fresh catch. My attention was especially attracted by the pollock, a slick, glossy cod sometimes caught in huge numbers and also called coalfish for its black skin. As death came to the fish, their life force bled away with a delicate, continuous shivering. Thousands and thousands of these fish were spread over the market like a quivering black carpet, framed into a square by the colorful stands of the flower sellers—a spectacle of deadly cheer.

I observed one particular market boy as he butchered hundreds of fish while flirting with a pretty serving girl. He grabbed the animals from a tub and slit their throats under the gills, without even glancing at them. This indifferent activity stood out in distressing contrast to the pain it caused. It was less the gruesomeness of the operation that created this impression than its mechanical inattentiveness. The movements of an indigenous fisherman I had watched cutting open and gutting his catch on a little bluff by Aicudia were infinitely more careful and attentive. Merchants handle their goods differently than hunters do their game.

During breakfast, it flashed through my mind that we have been born into a time in which we are simultaneously threatened by the industrious grabbing of the one and the accentuated cruelty of the other—a period of double consumption. Like Odysseus between Scylla and Charybdis, we navigate between wars and civil wars—and perhaps, like these fish, without even knowing the name of the process in whose nets we are entangled. How I would love to read about this in a history of the world that will appear in two hundred years. Unfortunately, such narratives often resemble books in which the dots on the *i* have been forgotten. Like the rich breakfast served at eleven here in the Bergen Fish Market, Paris of 1792 also offered pleasant diversions right next to the killing floors.

Historia in Nuce: The Wheel of Fortune — ***On Board***

Among all there is to observe at the annual fair are also the gatherings of people around the spinning wheel of fortune. Here we walk obliviously past one of the figures of destiny that order our lives—oblivious also of a wheel whose closer scrutiny would certainly benefit us, even if we missed out on the prizes promised by its comical barker.

We encounter these little mechanisms in various forms with a common operating principle. Their mechanics rely on the interplay of a wheel or turning disc with a system of symbols arranged as colors, numbers, or signs. Conceptually, we can visualize a wheel of fortune as composed of two circles: a fixed one marked with a graduated scale, and another whose function is simply to generate the cycles.

The game is simplified, but not changed, when the circle of symbols is united with that of the cycles. A normal roulette wheel that looks like a simple turntable has this form. But if we take a cross section of it, its dual nature emerges—we first make out a wheel, then a circle of symbols superimposed on it as slots or paintwork. There are also other forms of roulette in which the wheel turns but not the circle of symbols on which it makes its selection. This is the case for those wheels of fortune where the turntable has the form of a top, whose spinning propels a ball into peripheral slots. In this form, the game becomes clearer since the circle of symbols is fixed by its very nature and uniform in its divisions. This establishes a fixed win-loss ratio and thus an assured income for the enterprise for whom the wheel turns.

This process is reflected altogether differently in the gambler's world. For him, the turntable acquires tremendous meaning, since it creates the connection to that segment on the circle of symbols that represents his lot. A special feature called the index serves this purpose; it completes the wheel of fortune by qualifying the empty spinning of the turntable. At this point we are able to visualize an individual game by imagining a glass disc with an inscribed index revolving over a fixed circle of symbols. When the movement is interrupted, the index points to a segment on the circle of symbols and thus determines win or loss. It becomes apparent that the whole thing only becomes a real wheel of fortune with the addition of the index. It also explains the powerful intensification of a gambler's sense of life at the instant the marker stops on the circle of symbols.

In practice, the index appears in the most varied forms. We encounter it as a simple pointer, a rolling ball, and also as a pin or tooth that engages as a stopper with spokes or notches. In other cases, it functions as a projectile shot like a bolt onto the spinning wheel of fortune. An orphan reaching his hand into a rolling drum of lots performs an equivalent action—in all cases, it is a blind hit on the circle of symbols. The error all gamblers make is based on an optical illusion that makes the circle of symbols appear as a target, with the index as the aimed shot. They fancy that if they miss their number or symbol this time around, then their next shot will be that much more accurate. And so, when the little ball rolls, the playing room fills with tension, and every lucky gambler ascribes to himself a kind of paternity over his wins.

But far more significant relations than winning and losing are hidden in the wheel of fortune's construction; and the deep passion that its spinning arouses in a gambler's heart lies in the fact that it simultaneously operates as a perfect model of the turning of the world. Consequently, whenever man has looked to the stars for his fate, he has regarded the cosmos as a turning wheel of fortune, and the horoscope that the astrologer draws up for him represents nothing other than the circle of symbols, with his birth hour inscribed on it as the index. In contemplating this matter, a chill runs through us, aroused by the game of destiny.

We see the colorful, fixed circle of symbols with its unchanging divisions and over it, like a nebula, the empty cycle of time. Yet this spinning disc has enough room for all those who have ever lived, who will live, and who wait eternally in the womb of the unborn. They all play this game; and so a birth—and in equal measure its constellation—is one strike among millions. Justifiably then a man asks himself, be it in fortune or misfortune, that strange question: "Why *me* of all people?"

Our clocks are also built on the principle of the wheel of fortune, with these relations: the number dial plays the part of the circle of symbols, the wheel mechanism that of the turntable, and the hand that of the index. In order for the process to gain a qualitative character, it must be connected with our lot in life. The hands on the clocks in a watchmaker's shop move through the hours without relations, like a child's game involving imaginary roles. But when a buyer takes a clock home, it awakens to grave reality; now it will strike the hour for celebrations, for sorrows, and for trials. The bedside clocks of the sick are also supposed to stop at the moment of death. What a clock means to us in each case varies tremendously. A gambler clearly perceives it above all as a wheel of fortune. The hours are thus rich for him in unexpected windfalls, strokes of fate, changes, journeys, romantic trysts, and adventures of every kind. The other extreme is embodied by the kind of person who regards clocks as mere chronometers. Nonetheless, even he resembles a gambler, the kind that is satisfied with small, safe wins. Of course, even he must discover that his capital is not secure, even at the smallest interest rate, and that the "Una harum ultima"[62] inscribed on old clocks is true for him too. Wherever well-being is understood as a matter of luck, this difference falls away; a person who understands the great art of seizing the right moment will not retrospectively be examined about whether he determined it or simply guessed it. Incidentally, those who live strictly by the chronometer, such as functionaries, depend in their own special way on the movements of greater clocks of destiny.

It is also enlightening to recall the particular circumstances in which we acquired a new watch—we will discover that these days often coincide with those initiating new phases of our lives, days on which a new round in the game of life begins. The tall, chiming grandfather clock is

62. Many old clocks and sundials included some variation of this Latin phrase, which means "One of these [hours] will be the last."

part of the home and family, as the church clock is of the community. The custom of installing time wheels in high places—be it on clock towers or mountain peaks—goes back to the origins. Whether stone circles and sundials or Californian observatories, we find the circle of symbols in all of these. Of course, the questions man directs at the stars change, as do the answers.

But while a more profound gaze tries to investigate the unchanging fixed signs inscribed on the circle of symbols, a gloomy fear about the state of the world and a trembling in regard to destiny is connected with the moving part of the wheel and with the passage of time. The distinction between the lay and the initiated has always subsisted here; and the fixing of the circle of symbols was undoubtedly among the first priestly acts, along with the solitary sacrifice. This is shown by early altars, as well as by ancient fortune symbols and sun signs, which we can consider hieroglyphs of the circle of symbols and its delineated scale. In fixing the revolving spheres with a horoscope, the astrologer proceeds in the same manner as the initiate. Knowledge of the return, of the eternally alike, as revealed in the laying out of the calendar and its arrangement of feast days, belongs to this lore. Here lies the measure over which the lives, work, and daily whims of the people revolve, often passed down in the bones from priesthood to priesthood. The meaning of consecration is also revealed here, because it has always been a distinguishing trait of man to try to give the great moments of life a higher rank than that indicated by their mere dates. We all succumb to this inclination—not just the farmer in his fields, but also the mighty of this world, the victor in war and civil war, the legitimate sovereign as much as the usurper of power. All are moved by a passionate, secret desire: that their triumph represents fundamentally more than merely winning the jackpot from among millions of others, more than a lucky strike whose gains can be lost in the game of life with the next turn of the wheel. Such assurance can only exist where these dates are transferred, independently of time and its accidents, to the circle of unchanging order. Thus the lucky soldier reaching for the crown is ultimately satisfied neither by the power of acclamation nor by showy displays of his might. He shares this anxiety with the ordinary man, whose entry in the public registers leaves him dissatisfied, despite its certification of his marriage and baptism. A man believes nothing more certainly than that he lives an elect life, which goes beyond all chronological systems, and it is consecration that speaks to this belief.

Meditation on the wheel of fortune also provides good insights in individual cases. From these meditations, a hierarchy becomes visible in the writing of history. A man rises in this hierarchy to the degree that he can resist regarding history as a mere turning of the wheel. In this context, the chronological registration of facts occupies the lowest rung. But even it must have been preceded by a glance at the circle of symbols, since an awareness of the return of the eternally alike in time is the prerequisite of a year-count. Responsibility for the year counting itself fell early on to the cast of scribes, whose real work consisted of registration. Even today, during any process at a public counter, an essentially chronological act takes place; its index is the whack of the date stamp. From this point, there ensues under the most varying political configurations that commerce between the registering and consecrating powers which is one of history's great themes; and we observe a monument to it in the dual architecture of developed states.

Where our chronicles reach that highly developed state that makes them paragons for whole times and peoples, as with Tacitus for example, a special spiritual act is hidden in the act of registration. Here the representation of sequential events is preceded by an evaluation of their timeless significance. In this manner, history becomes transparent. This becomes wonderfully clear when such works accompany us over a lifetime. In youth, the once-off and chronological aspects contained in these works are clear to us. Later, however, the recurring aspects—that which is valid always and everywhere, including here and now—become more evident, the divine essence that conserves better than any stone or bronze. This epiphany comes to us above all once we have personally participated in historical world events. We could visualize historical ability as a net that only reaches a sufficient depth when the bronze of our own experience weighs it down. This is true even for quite superficial events; I remember only first really understanding the Law of the Maximum,[63] which I had often heard of, once I had lived through our own bout of inflation. Participation in the great

63. The Law of the Maximum was established during the French Revolution to set price limits, deter price gouging, and allow for a continued food supply to the people of France.

encounters belongs to our experiential capital to a far greater degree. This is related to the presence of a special disposition to the writing of history, which can often be detected in sovereigns, generals, and all those assigned important business. Undoubtedly it is an essentially secondary conjunction that exists here, since the ability to perceive unity in the convoluted puzzle of our efforts is necessarily reserved for the sovereign eye. Like the dispensation of justice, this is one of those domains in which achievements become more significant with age, all the way through to the years of senility that are detached from all interests. The function of seer also exists with respect to the past. This is all very clear with Dio Cassius,[64] and the passage in which he mentions divine duty is an especially beautiful one.

Beyond this, and superior to any kind of chronicle, there is a form of contemplation that endeavors to interpret the fixed signs underlying the cycles of time. A limited number of figures hide behind the plethora of the recurring. History becomes like a garden here, in which the eye sees, for the first time side-by-side, the flowers and fruits that are brought forth in constantly varying climates time and again by the flow of time. The extraordinary pleasure aroused by involvement with these works derives from our perceiving while in a stationary condition that which only otherwise emerges in motion, for instance the state in Aristotle's *Politics*. Incidentally, the figure of Aristotle himself provides a model of how men of destiny illuminate—because when the world is in order, the leading thinker of a period must necessarily also be the mentor of the king. The most recent relationship of this nature was that between Frederick the Great and Voltaire.

This form of history is the highest that the mind as observer can bring forth—because only while it poetizes is it able to elaborate myth. History writing by contrast remains bound to consciousness, to the mighty force that simultaneously limits the mind and gives it the power of a light ray. As the eye sees through the clearest waters to the amphorae and columns resting on the seabed, so a liberated vision can penetrate to the grounds of time, deep below ebb and flood. A question is resolved here, which even prominent historians have answered in the

64. Lucius Cassius Dio Cocceianus (c. AD 150–235), a Roman consul and historian of Rome.

negative—whether history belongs to the exact sciences. It can be answered affirmatively, if we recognize that the fixed signs lie below their fluid reflections, immutable in their relationships, like the axes and angles in a crystal.

The Echo of Images *Rio*

Since dawn, I had been prowling around in this sun god's residence, whose rocky gateway receives the stranger like the pillars of Hercules, beyond which he forgets the Old World. I had combed the markets and harbor quarters and walked along the grand boulevards to the outer suburbs where hummingbirds go to visit the large blossoms in the gardens. Then I returned via avenues lined with royal palms and flamboyants to the crowded city quarters and eavesdropped on the bustling and leisurely walks of life.

I awakened only in the late afternoon, as if from a dream during which I had forgotten to eat and drink, and I felt my spirit beginning to flag under the glut of images. Nevertheless, I could not detach myself and became a miser with my time. I allowed myself no break, but turned off into ever-new streets and squares.

Soon however it seemed that my steps had again lightened and the city had begun to transform in a curious way. Simultaneously, my way of seeing changed—whereas until then I had expended my observations on the new and unknown, now the images returned playfully to me. They were also now familiar to me, appearing as memories, as compositions of my self. I orchestrated my caprices as it pleased me with this game, like someone strolling around with a conductor's baton and making music with the world by pointing it now here, now there.

I felt at home with rich and poor, and the beggar who approached did me a service by providing an opportunity to verify this. At those vantage points where the city's amphitheater form is apparent, I realized that although an edifice like this is indeed plastered together by many generations, as if by bees, at the same time, a spirit brings it into being like the dream of a single night, and not for human habitation alone. Pearl oysters are also built of layers, but their value does not lie therein.

I reflected on these relationships in the evening at a café on the Copacabana. It appeared to me that an echo exists not only for the ear, but also for the eye—and the images we observe also return as a rhyme. As there are especially favorable conditions for every kind of echo, so it is beauty that echoes back most powerfully here.

But more simply and fundamentally, the matter is thus: with every deep and heartfelt glance that we direct at images, we make an offering, and according to our gift, so are we elevated.

The Fishmonger ***Ponta Delgada***

The Azores: a chain of volcanoes rising up on the outer fringe of Europe. I had been out and about since early morning, in gardens where the eye beholds the flowers of a new world, in fields surrounded by dark lava walls, and in tall forests of laurel. Only with the sun high in the sky did I head back to the harbor.

The streets lay quiet in the midday light; I heard only a gay, frequently repeated call in the distance, and I was taken by the whim to follow it. I soon came upon a tattered fellow carrying a load of already stiffened fish up and down the narrow, lifeless streets that hardly a dragon tree or araucaria lent their shadow to. I followed closely behind him, without him noticing, and his wonderfully vocalic call enchanted me. He shouted out an unknown Portuguese word—perhaps the name of the fish he was carrying. However, it seemed to me that he very quietly added something else; I therefore drew so close behind him that I was like his shadow.

Indeed, I now heard that as he ended his resounding call, he whisperingly muttered something else—a hungry prayer, or a weary curse? For no one stepped out of the houses and no windows opened.

We plodded on like this a long while through the hot alleys, offering fish that no one wanted at midday. And I listened a long while to his two voices, the loud and resonant, exuberantly soliciting call, and the quietly despairing soliloquy. I followed him like an avid eavesdropper, because I sensed that this was no longer about fish but rather that I was hearing the melody of man on this lost island—his simultaneously strutting and softly imploring tune.

Sicilian Letter to the Man in the Moon*

1.

Hail, you magician and friend of magicians! Friend of the lonely. Friend of heroes. Friend of the good and the evil. Confidant of nightly secrets. Tell me: where there is a confidant, is there not already more than can be known?

Well do I remember the hour in which your face appeared, large and terrible, in the window. Your light fell into the room like the phantom sword that freezes all motion as it is drawn. When you rise over the broad realms of stone, you see us slumbering, packed together with pallid faces, like numberless white pupae lying in the cells and corridors of an ant city, while a night wind sweeps through the great forests of fir above. Do we not live in an ocean abyss for you, creatures of the deep sea, but even deeper submerged than them?

So too the little room where I sat up in bed seemed submerged, immersed in a solitude too profound to be breached by others. All things stood silent and still in the alien light, like sea creatures glimpsed through a curtain of algae on the seabed. Did they not seem mysteriously transformed—and is transformation not the mask behind which the secret of life and death hides? Who is not familiar with such moments of nebulous anticipation, when we listen expectantly for an utterance from an unknown that yet seems close, when each form barely still manages to keep locked up what is hidden within it? A creaking in the woodwork, the ringing of a wine glass that an invisible hand seems

* Originally published as "Sizilianischer Brief an den Mann im Mond," in *Mondstein: Magische Geschichten*, ed. Franz Schauwecker (Berlin: Frundsberg, 1930), pp. 7–21. The piece was inspired by a hiking expedition to Sicily, which Jünger undertook with Hugo Fischer, his brother Friedrich Georg, and his wife Gretha from April 18 to May 5, 1929.

to have brushed by—how the space is charged by the efforts of a being that hungers for the means to pick up these cues!

Language has taught us to hold things in too much contempt. Great words are like the coordinates that we lay over a map. But is not a simple fistful of earth greater than an entire world that lies on a map? At one time, the murmuring of forms without name still had a weirder, more compelling ring. There are signs scratched on dilapidated fences and crossroad posts, which the townspeople walk heedlessly by. But the vagabond has an eye for them, he is studied in their lore; they are keys that reveal to him the essence of a whole territory, its dangers and its havens.

The child too is such a vagabond, who only recently crossed through the dark gate that separates us from our timeless homeland. And so it can still read in things the language of runes, which tells of a deeper brotherhood of Being.

2.

I feared you then, as a being of malevolent, magnetic power, and I imagined I could not stare into your full radiance without being robbed of gravity and sucked out, irresistibly, into empty space. Occasionally, I dreamt I let my guard slip, and then I saw myself in a long white shirt, driven involuntarily like a cork on a sinister tide, high over a landscape where gloomy forests lurked in the depths, where the roofs of the villages, castles, and churches glimmered like black silver—like the directly apprehensible sign language of a menacing geometry.

On these dream journeys, my body was quite rigid, with toes curled down, fists closed, head bent forward onto the chest. I felt no fear, only a sensation of inescapable loneliness in the midst of an extinguished world mysteriously governed by silent, secret powers.

3.

How this picture later changed under the influence of the northern lights, whose first irruption our proud and fiery heart suffers like a raging fever. There is a time when we are ashamed of our intoxications,[1] and another when we again acknowledge them. And we also do not like

1. *Rausch* has complex, multiple meanings for Jünger that include but go beyond the usual senses of "intoxication," "inebriation," and "being high"; he also uses the term to indicate states of revelatory ecstasy, rapture, or exaltation. Where it appears in the

to forgo the rapture of understanding[2] in its supreme boundlessness—because each of life's victories holds something absolute, because there is an enlightening deeper than the Enlightenment—because in it too a spark of the eternal light and a shadow of the eternal darkness hide.

Dark assault on the infinite! Should a brave heart be ashamed of taking part? Soldierly solitude of the mine saps, in which the work is done by seconds and millimeters, mighty front line of the trenches in no man's land, armed with rigorously calculated ramparts and sentry posts, with flashing machines and fantastical instruments!

Our thought lingers gladly at the border where number dissolves into symbol, circles gladly around infinity's two symbolic poles, the atom and the star—and it loves taking spoils on the battlefield of endless possibilities. What magician's apprentice never once stood behind the artificial predatory eye of a telescope moving with the course of soundless clocks in cosmic trajectories, never once belonged to the bustling throng of psychologists?

The danger gets very real here; and every lover of danger loves to respond to it. He wants to be attacked with greater ferocity, so that he can reply more ferociously in turn. The light appears more obscure by day than by night. Those who have tasted doubt are destined to seek the marvelous not here but beyond the frontiers of the intelligible. And anyone who has once doubted must doubt still more thoroughly to escape despair. Whether an individual is able to see in the infinite a number or a symbol? This is the one and only touchstone that reveals the nature of a spirit. But each of us has a different position to win, before he is capable of choosing. Happy is the simplicity that does not know the forked paths of doubt—yet a wilder, more virile happiness blooms on the edge of the abyss.

In any case—was it not surprising to discover that a light and shadow play of mountains, plains, dried-up seas, and extinct volcanoes lay behind the man in the moon? Here I remember Svidrigailov's curious suspicion—that eternity is merely a bare, whitewashed chamber, whose corners are populated with black spiders. One is led therein—and that is it, all there is to eternity.

text, it has been translated as seems most fitting. (See also his long, as yet untranslated essay *Annäherungen: Drogen und Rausch* [*Approaches: Drugs and Inebriation*].)

2. *Verstandesrausch*: rapture of understanding.

Indeed, and why not? What does the air matter to him who breathes it? What does transcendence matter to him for whom nothing exists that is not already transcendent?

What is needed is a new topography.

4.

A drill thinks in a different manner than a pair of pliers, which grasps the points one after another. Its thread cuts a swath through the various layers of the material, but all of the many points that it touches in this spiraling progression give direction and force to the thrust of the tip.[3] This relationship between chance and necessity, which do not exclude but rather depend on each other, is also inherent in the words and images of any language that aspires to the ultimate possibilities of understanding. Each word turns on an axis, which itself is incapable of bearing words. This language that I dream of must be intelligible, or utterly unintelligible, to the very last of its letters, as an expression of the supreme isolation that alone makes us capable of supreme love. There are also crystals that are only transparent in one direction.

But are you not yourself a master in setting artful riddles, whose texts alone are communicable but not their solutions, just as a hunter can tie fine nooses but must then wait in hope of game to draw them closed.

The solution need not be seen, only the riddle itself.

5.

You know the life that thrives at the edges of the dark forests, the gardens, islands illuminated by the gleam of lanterns and encircled in a magical whirl of music. You know the couples that silently disappear into the darkness; your rays strike their pale, mask-like faces, as lust hastens their breath and fear stifles it. And you know the inebriated ones who push alone through the undergrowth.

You rose large over the thatched house by the river on that night in June when one of your apprentices entered into a closer brotherhood with you. The drinking table was set on the trampled threshing floor, and in the haze of tobacco the weapons and red caps gleamed on the

3. Jünger's note: "The motion of the screw, crooked or straight, is one and the same."—Heraclitus

walls lined with fir branches. Where has the boyhood disappeared that so early broke open the secret seal of death, whose tidings already lay prepared for him? Youth was only once, and it is forever present. How our first inebriation pulls like sails on our heart! And was he also not dear to you when he sank for the first time into those depths where the elemental spirit so powerfully exhilarates us? Are there not hours when we cannot be but loved by everything around us, like a flower blooming in untouched innocence? Hours when the sheer excess squeezes us like a shot from our habitual paths? Only then do we begin to fly, and only in uncertainty is there a higher goal.

I follow him with my eyes, as if it just happened today, for there are experiences of a validity that eludes all the laws of time. When the wine's fire melts the growth rings that have encircled this strange heart, we discover that in the deep we have always remained the same. O remembrance, key to the innermost form that inhabits man and experience! Surely you are also present in the dark, bitterly intoxicating wine of death, that last and decisive triumph of Being over Existence. You solitary revelers I greet before all others, you who keep your own company at table and raise your glass time and time again to your own honor! What are we but mirror images of our selves, and where we sit like this as two, there the third, the god, is also not far.

I see your protégé as he appears from out of a furious cloud of noise at the low door over which the narrow, white horse's skull gleams bright in the night light. The warm air, laden with grass pollen as though with narcotic gunpowder, elicits a wild outburst that drives him shouting, blundering, into the silent landscape. He dashes along the top of the high wall that borders the meadow, then falls from it, curiously without pain, into the thick grass. He races onward, with a sense of power that seems fueled by boundless resources. The great white umbels that glide by like alien signs, the smell of the hot, fermenting earth, the bitter vapors of wild carrot and spotted hemlock—all these like the pages of a book that opens of itself and gives word of ever-deeper and more miraculous relationships. No more thought, the attributes melt darkly into each other. Nameless life is jubilantly hailed.

He breaks into the broad belt of reeds along the stream. Gas bubbles up from the mud. The water enfolds his glowing breast with arms, and then his face glides off over the dark mirror of the river. A weir thunders in the distance, and the ear, now near to the primal language, feels itself dangerously enticed. From the bottomless depths, the stars glimmer up and begin to dance in the water's swirls and eddies.

On the far bank, the forest opens up; its undergrowth entraps life in menacing, snarled lines. The roots spread out their intertwined arrays of threads and tentacles, and the branches lace themselves into a net, on whose fringe a host of faces move and change. Lattices of blind, generative power intersect overhead, their forms spawning antagonism and downfall together, and at the foot of the trees, the dreary vapors of decay swirl up, in which life mingles muddily with death.

But then a clearing opens up, and your radiance falls into the darkness like a thunderbolt of the law. The trunks of the beeches gleam like silver, the oaks like the dark bronze of which the old swords were wrought. Their crowns loom in mighty formations. Every last twig and blackberry stalk is touched by your light, interpreted and disclosed, as it is enclosed—touched by a grand moment that confers meaning on everything and ambushes chance on its secret paths. All belongs to an equation whose unfamiliar symbols are written in glowing ink.

How the simple lines of the homeland are hidden in even the most convoluted of territories! Happy allegory, in which a yet deeper one is rooted.

6.

What is it that sustains us, if not that mysterious ray of light that sometimes flashes through our inner wilderness? A man will speak, however imperfectly, of that which is more than human in him.

The efforts of science to contact distant stars are an important trait of our times. We are captivated by the strange mixture of sobriety and fantasy that characterizes not just the efforts themselves, but also their technical methods. Is it not an astonishing proposal to represent a right-angled Pythagorean triangle with its three quadrants in beacon lights over the Sahara? What does it matter if there is a mathematician somewhere out there in the universe! For here is a real living feature that calls to mind the language of the pyramids, an echo of the holy origins of art, of the solemn lore of creation in its secret sense—with all the premises of abstract thought brought into harmony and disguised by modern technics.

Will they ever be received, these radio signals that we launch into the icy, bottomless depths of space—this translation of languages, already bounded by terrestrial mountains and rivers, into electrical impulses that plead admission at the very borders of infinity? And into what language will this translation be translated?

Wondrous Tibetans, whose monotone prayers ring out from the cliff-top monasteries of the observatories! Who could laugh at a prayer wheel who is familiar with our own landscapes with their myriad of spinning wheels—with the furious commotion that moves the hour hands of all our clocks and the racing crankshafts of airplanes? Sweet and dangerous opium of speed!

But is it not true that stillness hides at the absolute center of the wheel? Stillness is the primal language of speed. And by whatever transformations we may wish to increase speed, they can all be no more than translations of this primal language. But how should man understand his own language?

Behold! You look down on our cities. Before these you have seen many other kinds of cities, and will see many others yet. Each single house is well constructed and built for its own special purpose. There are narrow, winding streets that seem to have been laid out by pure chance in the course of time, like fields in a farming region that are divided up according to long-forgotten inheritances. Others again are straight and wide, aligned by princes and master architects. The fossils of eras and races interpenetrate in many different ways. The geology of the human soul is a particular science. Life pursues its course between the churches and state buildings, the villas and tenement blocks, the bazaars and pleasure palaces, the train stations and industrial zones; the traffic is considerable, but the solitude prodigious.

But from your great height, this vast accumulation of organic and mechanical power takes on a different aspect. Even an eye observing it through the keenest telescope could not fail to notice the great difference. Though the reality is not changed for the viewer, a different side comes to the fore. And so, from this distant perspective, the differences between the eras melt into each other. It is no longer apparent that the churches and castles are thousands of years old, the warehouses and factories only from yesterday; instead something emerges that could be called their pattern—the common crystalline structure in which the basic material has deposited itself. Even the incalculable diversity of purposes and movements that are generated is no longer perceptible. Two people hurry by each other down there, two worlds unto themselves, and one city quarter can be more distant from the next than the north and south poles. But from your perspective, you as cosmic being and yet still part of the earth, this is all perceived in stillness, almost like something discharged by volcanic fermentation and the ephemeral fluids of life. O marvelous, and ever again marvelous spectacle, as form upon forms arise from the antagonisms of times and places. This is what I call the deeper fraternity of life, which integrates all antagonisms.

But rarely is it permitted us down here to see purpose fused with meaning. And yet our highest aspiration must be the stereoscopic glance that grasps things in their more secret and dormant physicality. The necessary is a special dimension. We live inside that necessity, and yet are only capable of beholding its projections, and even then only in the most significant part of our being. There are signs, metaphors, and keys of many kinds—and we are like the blind, who, though unable to see, can still sense the light in its duller quality, as warmth.

And is it not true, that although a blind person remains eternally shrouded in darkness, his every movement takes place in the light for one who sees? So we too have never contemplated our faces in mirrors of a more timeless quality. And we also speak a language whose meanings even we have no insight into—a language whose every syllable is at once transitory and eternal. Symbols are signs, which nevertheless give us an awareness of our value. First, they are projections of forms from a hidden dimension, but then also floodlights by which we launch our signals into the unknown in a language pleasing to the gods. And these enigmatic conversations, this sequence of prodigious aspirations that form the core of our history, which is a history of the battles of men and gods - - -: only they make humanity worthy of study.

7.

True comparison, that is, the contemplation of things according to their place on the plane of necessity, is the most marvelous method of marksmanship. Its base is the common expression of the essential, and its peak is the essential itself.

This is a form of higher trigonometry, which concerns itself with the measuring of invisible fixed stars.

8.

On this bright morning, I climbed up into the ravines of Monte Gallo.[4] The red-brown earth of the gardens was still moist with dew, and the red and yellow flowers of the Saracen spring spread out under the lemon trees like a pattern woven into an oriental rug. Where the top leaves of the prickly pears peeked naked and curious over the ruddy wall, the mountain meadows began, towered over by cliffs and ablaze with yellow spurge shrubs. Then the path led through a narrow valley carved from the barren rock.

I do not know and will not attempt to describe how, between these walls, the insight suddenly emerged that a valley like this, with its stony language, more insistently seizes the wanderer than is possible in a more pristine landscape, or, put otherwise, that a landscape like this has deeper powers at its disposal. Though this must have always been evident to every mind of higher rank, yet the moments are rare when we are confronted with a physical manifestation—and not just the cognition—of the ensouled life that exists in nature. Indeed, I believe they have only recently become possible again. But it was just such a moment that took me by surprise at that hour—I sensed the eyes of the valley resting their full attention on me. In other words: it was beyond any doubt that the valley had its daemon.

Just then, still in the rapture of discovery, my gaze fell on your now very pale disk in the sky, which could still be seen—probably only from down here below—just over the high ridgeline. There, in a lightning-fast birth, the image of the man in the moon emerged again. Now it is certainly true that the lunar landscape with its rocks and valleys is a surface that creates a task for astronomical topographers. But it is equally certain that it is simultaneously accessible to the magical trigonometry mentioned earlier—that it is at the same time a domain of spirits, and that the fantasy that gave it a face understood the primal text of the runes and the language of daemons with all the profundity of a child's glance. But what was unprecedented for me in this moment was to see

4. A mountain rising above Palermo.

these two masks of one and the same Being melt inseparably into each other. Because here, for the first time, a tormenting dichotomy resolved itself for me, which I, as great-grandson of an idealistic, grandson of a romantic, and son of a materialistic generation, had until then held to be irresolvable. It was not that an Either/Or changed into a Both/And. No, the real is just as magical as the magical is real.

Here it was, the miraculous quality that had delighted us about the twofold images that we observed as children through a stereoscope: in the very moment that they fused together into a single image, a new dimension of depth emerged from within them.

And so it is indeed: time has brought the old magical spells, which were long forgotten but ever-present, close to us again. We sense how meaning begins to flow, still tentatively, into the grand work we are all creating and that holds us all in its spell.

Also from Telos Press Publishing

The Non-Philosophy Project:
Essays by François Laruelle
Gabriel Alkon and Boris Gunjevic, eds.

The Democratic Contradictions of Multiculturalism
Jens-Martin Eriksen and Frederik Stjernfelt

A Journal of No Illusions:
Telos, *Paul Piccone, and the Americanization of Critical Theory*
Timothy W. Luke and Ben Agger, eds.

Hamlet or Hecuba:
The Intrusion of the Time into the Play
Carl Schmitt

Class Cleansing: The Massacre at Katyn
Victor Zaslavsky

On Pain
Ernst Jünger

Confronting the Crisis: Writings of Paul Piccone
Paul Piccone

Jihad and Jew-Hatred:
Islamism, Nazism, and the Roots of 9/11
Matthias Küntzel

Theory of the Partisan
Carl Schmitt

The Nomos *of the Earth*
in the International Law of the Jus Publicum Europaeum
Carl Schmitt